QUICK & EASY COOKING

DELICIOUS MEALS IN UNDER 60 MINUTES

QUICK & EASY COOKING

DELICIOUS MEALS IN UNDER 60 MINUTES

Pamela Westland

CONTENTS

ANOTHER BEST-SELLING VOLUME FROM HPBooks®
Publisher: Rick Bailey; Editorial Director: Elaine R. Woodard
Editor: Jeanette P. Egan; Art Director: Don Burton
Book Assembly: Leslie Sinclair
Typography: Cindy Coatsworth, Michelle Carter
Book Manufacture: Anthony B. Narducci
Recipe testing by International Cookbook Services: Barbara Bloch,
President; Rita Barrett, Director of Testing; Marina Freyer, Tester

Published by HPBooks, Inc.
P.O. Box 5367, Tucson, AZ 85703 602/888-2150
ISBN 0-89586-342-1
Library of Congress Catalog Card Number 85-60086
© 1985 HPBooks, Inc. Printed in the U.S.A.
1st Printing

Originally published as The Busy Cook's Book
© 1983 Hennerwood Publications Limited

Cover Photo: Ham & Cheese Crepes, page 58

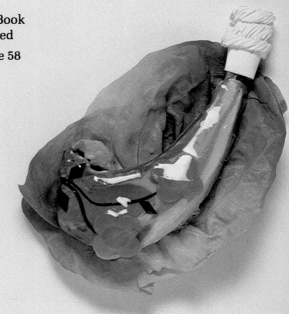

Introduction

Preparing and cooking a meal for family and friends is an exciting challenge—and one which this book will help you meet successfully, again and again. Whether you are looking for speedy new ideas for family snacks, need inspiration when you have only minutes between dashing home and serving a meal, or want something simple yet impressive to offer your guests—read on!

The title has been taken literally. Recipes were chosen and written to be quick and easy. Preparation time may vary according to your expertise, but the times listed can be used as planning guides. At a glance, you can choose the chapter to suit the occasion—whether you have fifteen, thirty, forty-five or sixty minutes; want to prepare one dish or a complete meal in advance; or want a balanced menu already planned for you.

Inventory your kitchen equipment occasionally to see if replacements or new items are needed. Take good care of nonstick cooking surfaces. Keep appliances in good working order. Make sure that everything is conveniently located. Just moving your most frequently used gadgets from one drawer to another nearer the sink or range, and making space for the mixer on the countertop, can save steps and time. Adding a few inexpensive tools could be the key to more leisure time over the years.

KITCHEN EQUIPMENT

Knives—Choose the best you can afford and keep them sharp. Non-stainless-steel knives remain sharp longer. You need straight-edged blades for chopping, dicing and shredding. Scalloped- or serrated-edged ones are best for the sawing motion needed to slice bread, meat, frozen foods, fruit and vegetables, especially those with tough skins, like tomatoes. Use stainless-steel knives for cutting acidic foods, such as lemons.

Hand tools—Time-savers include: good-quality kitchen scissors for snipping everything from marshmallows to chives; an apple corer, which also cuts decorative butter pats and carrots slices; a slicer to cut wafer-thin slices of vegetables that will cook quickly or to slice cucumbers for salads; a fruit zester to scrape rapidly across lemon and orange peel; a wire whisk to leave the other hand free for pouring; a stiff vegetable brush to brush along the grain to clean celery and to scrub root vegetables; and a salad spinner to make short work of drying lettuce and other salad greens.

Weights and measures—A set of accurate kitchen scales may be helpful. Standard measuring cups for dry and liquid ingredients and a set of standard measuring spoons are essentials for kitchen success. Extra sets of these are handy when making several recipes at once.

Utensils—Flameproof casseroles save time and dishwashing. The casserole can be used on the stove top and in the oven, as well as on the table. One-pot cooking was invented for the busy cook! Nonstick pans and bakeware of all kinds make flipping, tossing and turning easier.

Again, buy the best you can afford. This is where quality really counts.

ELECTRICAL EQUIPMENT

Blenders crumb bread and cookies, grate nuts and cheese, make fruit and vegetable purees, stir batters and sauces and make creamy pâtés and foolproof mayonnaise.

Electric mixers, with their many speeds and attachments, whip, whisk, cream, beat, chop, slice, shred, mince, grind and sieve.

Food processors, with the various discs, cope with almost every step of food preparation except beating egg whites, whipping cream and sieving foods.

Slow-cookers cook casseroles, puddings, stews, soups and vegetables slowly and surely. This is a perfect way to cook at a controlled temperature when you are away from home.

Pressure cookers, the original fast-cookers, are especially time-saving for less-tender cuts of meat, root vegetables, dried beans and peas and steamed puddings. Foods which take a long time to cook can have cooking time reduced by half when cooked in a pressure cooker.

Steamers and rice cookers cook rice and keep it hot. Rice cookers will soft-cook or hard-cook eggs to perfection. Steamers and rice cookers also steam meat, fish, fruit and vegetables.

Microwave ovens are useful for cooking foods quickly. They also can be used to defrost frozen items and to reheat leftovers. Many models offer features that make cooking practically foolproof. As with any electrical appliance, follow the manufacturer's directions. There is cookware on the market that can be used in both microwave and conventional ovens. Check labels to be sure. Many conventional recipes can be adapted for the microwave oven.

THINGS TO HAVE ON HAND

It's reassuring to keep a carefully chosen stock of the canned, packaged and frozen foods you use most often. Here are some reminders.

Canned goods—Peeled tomatoes are time savers for sauces, soups and casseroles. Consommé makes a good instant soup with a dash of sherry and a tastier beef stock than bouillon cubes. The condensed kind doubles for a meat glaze and, when chilled, can be chopped and mixed with cold meats, even melon, as a salad. Tuna turns green salad into a French-style meal and makes a marvelous sauce for pasta or rice or a filling for pastry. All canned fruits are useful; some are more versatile than others. For example, grapefruit sections mixed with sliced avocado make a great salad in a hurry. Peach or apricot halves broiled or baked with a stuffing take on a touch of glamour that belie their usual image.

Dry goods—Check stocks regularly, or store in clear containers so you can tell at a glance when to buy more. Add variety with brown and white rice and whole-wheat and vegetable pasta in all shapes and sizes. Choose from a wide selection of dried legumes. Try lentils, red kidney beans, pinto beans or navy beans; reduce the cooking time by cooking in a pressure cooker.

Frozen foods—Keep a selection of frozen vegetables in your freezer to add variety in shape and color to your meals. Broccoli, green peas, carrots, corn, green beans, spinach and even potatoes will add a quick side dish.

Quick-thawing fruits, such as raspberries, strawberries, blueberries and peaches, make easy desserts. Ice cream can be a dessert by itself, or serve it with cookies, cake or fruit. Frozen pie crust and puff pastry save time; bake and add a filling for a dessert in minutes. Keep yeast rolls in the freezer. Or, freeze yeast dough; bake before guests arrive to give your kitchen that warm, delicious aroma of home-baked bread. Freeze foods in serving sizes that are right for your family. It's easy to open two packages for guests.

HELPFUL HINTS

● A day or two in advance, chop herbs for garnishes; slice or chop mushrooms, onions or carrots. Do not chop vegetables such as potatoes that turn brown. Store prepared vegetables in tightly covered containers in the refrigerator.
● Section or slice oranges and grapefruit; squeeze orange juice or lemon juice. Grate citrus peel up to 2 days ahead.
● Make sugar syrup for fruit salad; add a bay leaf or orange-peel twist. Refrigerate up to 4 days.

● Use small, clean containers with lids for storing prepared items. But, remember to label them clearly. A frantic last-minute search for chopped parsley saves neither time nor temper!
● Make extra cookies, sheet cakes or pie crusts; freeze for an easy dessert later.
● Chop or grind nuts. Toast nuts while using the oven or broiler. Store nuts in tightly covered containers in the refrigerator.
● Prepare two casseroles at the same time—one to serve and one to freeze for later. This saves preparation and cleanup time.
● When measuring honey or syrup, use the cup to measure the shortening first. The honey or syrup will slide out easily.
● Dip peaches or tomatoes into boiling water for a few seconds before peeling them.
● Never waste anything. Make stock from bones left from deboning a roast or chicken. Combine bones, chopped onion, carrots, celery and herbs in a large stockpot. Simmer 1 to 2 hours. Cool and strain. Freeze up to 3 months.
● Use leftover wine and spices to poach apples or pears. Or, use wine instead of water in sugar syrup for extra-special fruit salads. Wine can also be frozen in ice-cube trays.
● A heat diffuser that fits over a heating unit on the range allow you to simmer stews and casseroles on very low heat. This frees you to do other things without worrying

Ingredients for garnishes

that your dish will burn.
● To cool hot foods quickly, place container in a larger pan or sink of cold water. Be careful that the water does not enter the food. Or, pour liquid foods into a shallow pan to cool more quickly.

Handy Equivalents	
1 cup uncooked white rice	= 3 cups cooked rice
1 cup uncooked brown rice	= 3 to 4 cups cooked rice
1 cup uncooked quick-cooking rice	= 1 to 2 cups cooked rice
1 cup uncooked dried beans	= about 2 cups cooked beans
1 (15-oz.) can beans	= about 2 cups cooked beans
1 cup uncooked noodles	= 1-1/2 cups cooked noodles
1 cup unwhipped whipping cream	= 2 cups whipped cream
1 cup self-rising flour	= 1 cup all-purpose flour plus 1-1/2 teaspoons baking powder and 1/2 teaspoon salt

IN FIFTEEN MINUTES

Rushing in from work or shopping? Unexpected guests to cook for? What can you cook in fifteen minutes? Lots of things, from simple dishes like *Pan-Fried Danish Egg & Bacon* and *Apple Stacks*, to really super main dishes that are fit for a party. You will enjoy trying *Shrimp in Garlic Butter* or *Steak with Anchovies*.

When time is so precious, it's best to spend it all on the main dish and keep the side dishes simple. Quick-cooking rice and pasta come to the rescue.

And for dessert? Even as the minutes tick away, there's time for *Banana & Rum Flambé*, chilled *Raspberry Cream* or *Ginger-Soufflé Omelet*. All in fifteen minutes or less!

IN THIRTY MINUTES

After cooking a main dish in a quarter of an hour, thirty minutes seems quite a luxury! Using quick-cooking meats, such as pork tenderloin, ham steaks, liver or fish fillets, you can produce tempting meals. The secret is in simple, but good, sauces. These include *Orange & Ginger Sauce*, *Pimento Mayonnaise* and *Cucumber Sauce*. The little extras make all the difference; recipes include herbs, spices and flavored butters for cooking and glazing.

Wrapping food in foil reduces cleanup time. Try foil-wrapped *Sole & Mushrooms in Sweet & Sour Sauce*.

Fresh fruit is a positive boon when time is at a premium.

Peach Caramels and *Poached Pears with Chocolate Sauce* are two more ideas for glamorous presentations.

IN FORTY-FIVE MINUTES

In this amount of time, there is an opportunity to use the oven, to prepare fresh vegetables and to make warm and welcome desserts. Mixing and matching these ideas, you can easily prepare two courses well within your deadline. While thin, tender beef strips are cooking in red wine, you could make *Honey Cream*. With *Blue-Cheese Soufflé* in the oven, *Peaches in Marmalade Sauce* could be sizzling to spicy perfection at the same time.

A few extra minutes spent in preparing a dish can more than pay dividends when it comes to cooking. Cut vegetables into flowerets or slices. Cut meat into small strips, or use prepared chicken or turkey cutlets. Reducing the size of the food also reduces the cooking time.

IN SIXTY MINUTES

An hour to produce a main dish or a complete meal gives you a little breathing space. It gives you time to prepare the dish and start it cooking. You can set the table, put away the groceries or do last-minute picking up before guests arrive. The recipes in this chapter do not require your full attention while they cook.

While the *Honeyed Lamb* is cooking to succulence, you have time to make a batch of crepes for *Crepe Gâteau with Cherry Sauce*. While the brown rice is simmering to a delicious nutty tenderness and the vegetables are steaming, there's plenty of time to whip up a dessert from one of the earlier chapters. And while a tangy *Steamed Lemon & Raisin Pudding* is steaming away, you could be turning your attention to one of the quick broiled or pan-fried dishes.

AHEAD OF TIME

Some of the dishes in this chapter, such as the *Pickled Herring* and *Coriander Lamb*, can be made more than a day ahead. As with all spiced dishes, making ahead is a positive advantage because it allows the flavors to blend and mellow. Another plus: meat actually tenderizes as it spends this extra time marinating in its sauce.

Cooking ahead of time does not imply that you have all the time in the world, only that you use time more efficiently. Some dishes in this section, such as *Potted Ham* and *Blue-Cheese Mousse, Gingersnap-Cream Roll* and *Almond-Mint Pie*, are so snappy, they could be in the first two chapters. When you want to spend longer preparing a dish, there are recipes included that require more time and are worth the effort.

When moments count, don't stop at cooking and preparing the food ahead of time. Do everything ahead that you can. Set the table, or at least get out the china and silverware. Arrange condiments; make salad dressings. Don't forget to check salt and pepper shakers; fill if needed. No matter how little you do ahead, that little will be an enormous help. And just knowing that it is done—another thing ready and waiting—gives your confidence a boost. That's what enjoying serving a meal to family and friends is all about!

MENUS

When you are entertaining friends at lunch or dinner, it isn't always possible to spend as much time as you would like preparing and cooking the meal. Our menus make allowance for this. Each menu includes at least one course prepared ahead, reassuringly ready to serve or to finish at mealtime. In many cases this made-ahead dish is the first course. *Potato & Sausage Salad, Smoked Mackerel & Cream-Cheese Pâté* or *Pears with Camembert Sauce* are examples of this. Many of these starters have other possibilities, too. With crudités and a basket of hot, crusty rolls or a French-bread loaf, they make a perfect light lunch or supper dish.

In all menu planning, balance is the key word—balance of the nutritional values, colors, textures and flavors. Fruit and vegetables feature strongly in many of the menus; they add bright colors, crunchy textures and important vitamins and minerals. Cost is another consideration in meal planning. If one dish calls for an expensive ingredient, balance your budget by planning less-expensive side dishes.

Whether you plan a low-cost family supper or a special dinner for your guests, the same principles apply. This careful selection of dishes allows you more time to relax with family and friends. Last-minute attention to details in the kitchen is minimized.

In Fifteen Minutes

Shrimp in Garlic Butter

1/2 cup butter or margarine
1 medium onion, finely chopped
3 garlic cloves, finely chopped
12 oz. peeled, uncooked shrimp, thawed, if frozen
2 tablespoons chopped fresh parsley
Pinch of salt
Freshly ground black pepper
Pinch of red (cayenne) pepper
1/4 teaspoon lemon juice

To garnish:
1 lemon, quartered

Preparation and cooking time: 15 minutes

1. Melt butter or margarine in a medium skillet over medium heat. Add onion; sauté 4 minutes, stirring once or twice. Stir in garlic and shrimp; reduce heat to low. Cook over low heat 5 minutes, stirring occasionally.
2. Stir in 1/2 of parsley, salt, black pepper, red pepper and lemon juice.
3. Garnish with remaining parsley and lemon wedges. Serve hot with crusty rolls. Makes 4 servings.

Poached Trout

4 medium rainbow trout, ready to cook
1/2 cup white wine or cider
Few parsley sprigs
1 medium onion, sliced
2 lemon slices
6 peppercorns
1/2 cup whipping cream
Salt
Freshly ground pepper

To garnish:
Parsley sprigs

Preparation and cooking time: 15 minutes

1. In a skillet, combine trout, wine or cider, parsley, onion, lemon and peppercorns. Cover; simmer 10 minutes or until fish tests done. Place cooked trout on a platter; keep warm.
2. Strain cooking liquid into a small saucepan; bring to a boil. Immediately reduce heat; stir in cream. Heat until hot. Season sauce with salt and pepper.
3. Pour sauce over fish; garnish with parsley sprigs.
4. Serve with small new potatoes for a perfect accompaniment. Makes 4 servings.

Smoked-Mackerel & Orange Kabobs

1 cup quick-cooking rice
Salt
1 tablespoon butter or margarine
Juice and peel of 1/2 orange
4 medium smoked-mackerel fillets or other smoked-fish fillets, skinned
1 teaspoon lemon juice
Freshly ground pepper
3 large oranges, peeled, sectioned
2 tablespoons blanched almonds

To garnish:
1 bunch watercress, trimmed

Preparation and cooking time: 15 minutes

1. Cook rice according to package directions. Stir in salt, butter or margarine, orange juice and orange peel. Keep rice mixture warm.
2. Preheat broiler. While rice is cooking, cut fish fillets crosswise into 1-inch strips; toss strips in lemon juice. Sprinkle with pepper. Thread mackerel strips and orange sections alternately on 4 skewers. Broil under preheated broiler 5 minutes, turning skewers once.
3. Place almonds on a dry baking sheet; toast under broiler 2 minutes, turning once.
4. Immediately before serving, stir toasted almonds into rice. Place skewers on rice; garnish with watercress. Makes 4 servings.

Top to bottom: Poached Trout, Boiled potatoes, Smoked-Mackerel & Orange Kabobs

Pan-Fried Danish Egg & Bacon

6 bacon slices
4 large tomatoes, sliced
1/2 teaspoon Italian seasoning
1 teaspoon vegetable oil
1 tablespoon all-purpose flour
6 tablespoons milk
6 eggs
Salt
Freshly ground pepper
1 tablespoon butter or margarine

To garnish:
Parsley sprigs

Preparation and cooking time: 10 minutes

1. Preheat broiler. Place bacon on a broiler-pan rack. Broil under preheated broiler 2 minutes; turn slices.
2. Place tomatoes on rack with bacon; sprinkle tomato slices with 1/2 of Italian seasoning and oil. Broil 3 minutes. Keep warm.
3. While bacon and tomatoes are cooking, prepare eggs. Place flour in a medium bowl; stir in milk. Beat in eggs until blended. Stir in salt, pepper and remaining Italian seasoning.
4. Melt butter or margarine in a large skillet. Pour in egg mixture; cook over medium heat 4 to 5 minutes, lifting edges occasionally with a spatula.
5. When eggs are set, arrange broiled bacon in a wheel pattern on top with broiled tomatoes overlapping around edge. Garnish with parsley sprigs. Cut into quarters; serve hot. Makes 4 servings.

Pan-Fried Danish Egg & Bacon

Apple Stacks

Apple Stacks

4 large cooking apples
1/4 cup honey
3/4 cup shredded Cheddar cheese (3 oz.)
1/2 small head lettuce, shredded
2 tablespoons walnut halves

Preparation and cooking time: 15 minutes

1. Preheat broiler. Line a broiler pan with foil.
2. Peel and core apples; cut each crosswise into 3 or 4 rings. Arrange rings close together on foil; spread with 1/2 of honey.
3. Broil under preheated broiler 3 minutes. Using a spatula, turn apple rings; spread with remaining honey. Broil 3 minutes. Sprinkle cheese over apples; broil 2 minutes.
4. Stack cooked slices into 4 apple shapes; see below. Place lettuce on 4 plates. Place apples on lettuce; garnish with walnut halves. Makes 4 servings.

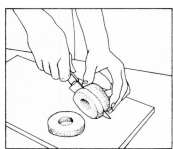
1/Cut apples crosswise into 3 or 4 slices.

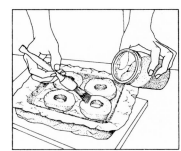
2/Spread with 1/2 of honey.

3/Sprinkle cheese over apples.

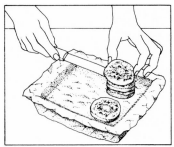
4/Stack cooked slices into 4 apple shapes.

Spaghetti with Cream Sauce

12 oz. whole-wheat spaghetti
Salt
1/4 cup butter or margarine
6 oz. button mushrooms, sliced
2 to 3 tablespoons chopped fresh herbs
Freshly ground pepper
1/2 pint whipping cream (1 cup)
2 egg yolks
1/2 cup shredded sharp Cheddar cheese (2 oz.)

Preparation and cooking time: 15 minutes

1. Cook spaghetti in boiling salted water according to package directions until tender.
2. While spaghetti is cooking, prepare sauce. Melt butter or margarine in a medium skillet. Add mushrooms; sauté over medium heat 3 minutes. Stir in 2 tablespoons herbs, salt and pepper; cook 1 minute.
3. In a medium saucepan, heat cream over low heat; do not boil. Beat in egg yolks; stir in cheese, salt and pepper.
4. Drain spaghetti; return to pan. Stir in mushroom mixture. Turn pasta into a warm serving dish; pour cream sauce over spaghetti. Sprinkle with remaining herbs, if desired. Serve immediately. Makes 4 servings.

Eggs with Blue-Cheese Mayonnaise

6 hard-cooked eggs
2/3 cup mayonnaise
1/2 cup crumbled Danish blue cheese (2 oz.)
1/4 cup soft farmer's cheese (2 oz.)
6 tablespoons whipping cream
Freshly ground pepper
1 small head lettuce
1 bunch watercress, trimmed
2 tablespoons chopped mint

To garnish:
2 tomatoes, quartered

Preparation: 15 minutes

1. Peel eggs; cut peeled eggs into halves.
2. In a small bowl, combine mayonnaise, cheeses and cream. Stir until blended; season with pepper.
3. Finely shred lettuce. In a medium bowl, combine shredded lettuce, watercress and mint.
4. Divide salad among 4 plates; arrange 3 egg halves on each plate, cut-sides down. Spoon mayonnaise mixture over eggs. Garnish with tomato wedges. Makes 4 servings.

Ham Steaks with Cucumber Sauce

2 smoked-ham center slices, about 1 lb. total weight
1 teaspoon vegetable oil

Cucumber Sauce:
1 medium cucumber, peeled, diced
Salt
1-1/2 tablespoons butter or margarine
3 tablespoons all-purpose flour
1 cup milk
2 tablespoons whipping cream
1 tablespoon chopped chives
Ground white pepper
Pinch of red (cayenne) pepper

Preparation and cooking time: 15 minutes

1. Preheat broiler. Brush ham with oil; place on a broiler-pan rack. Broil under preheated broiler 4 to 5 minutes per side. While ham is cooking, prepare sauce.
2. To prepare sauce, in a medium saucepan, cook cucumber in boiling salted water 3 minutes; drain thoroughly. Pat dry with paper towels.
3. In a medium saucepan, melt butter or margarine; stir in flour. Cook over medium heat 1 minute, stirring constantly. Gradually stir in milk; bring sauce to a boil. Simmer 3 minutes. Stir cooked cucumber, cream and chives into sauce. Season with salt, white pepper and red pepper.
4. Cut broiled ham into serving pieces. Arrange on a serving plate; spoon a little sauce over ham to garnish. Serve remaining sauce separately.
5. Serve with small new potatoes and a green vegetable, such as broccoli spears. Makes 4 servings.

Turkey in Sweet & Sour Sauce

1 lb. turkey breast
2 teaspoons cornstarch
2 tablespoons vegetable oil
1 tablespoon butter or margarine
4 oz. mushrooms, thinly sliced

Sweet & Sour Sauce:
6 tablespoons water
1-1/2 teaspoons cornstarch
1-1/2 tablespoons light-brown sugar
1-1/2 tablespoons honey
3 tablespoons red-wine vinegar
3 tablespoons tomato paste
3 tablespoons orange juice
3 tablespoons soy sauce

To serve:
About 2 cups hot cooked white rice

Preparation and cooking time: 15 minutes

1. Cut turkey into 5 (2-inch x 1/2-inch) strips. In a medium bowl, toss turkey strips with cornstarch.
2. Heat oil in a large skillet over medium heat. Add coated turkey strips; sauté 3 minutes. Remove from skillet with a slotted spoon; drain on paper towels. Melt butter or margarine in same skillet. Add mushrooms; sauté 2 minutes.
3. To prepare sauce, in a medium saucepan, combine water and cornstarch into a smooth paste. Stir in remaining ingredients. Bring sauce to a boil, stirring constantly. Simmer 1 minute; stir in drained turkey. Simmer 5 minutes.
4. Stir sautéed mushrooms into turkey mixture. Serve hot over rice. Makes 4 servings.

Liver with Fresh Sage

1 lb. calves' liver, cut into thin slices
1-1/2 tablespoons all-purpose flour
Salt
Freshly ground pepper
1/2 teaspoon rubbed sage or 1 teaspoon chopped fresh sage
2 tablespoons butter or margarine
1 tablespoon vegetable oil
About 12 fresh sage leaves
1/2 cup condensed consommé
1 teaspoon lemon juice
Hot cooked rice

To garnish:
4 sage sprigs

Preparation and cooking time: 15 minutes

1. Cut liver slices into 1/2-inch strips. In a plastic bag, combine flour, salt, pepper and rubbed sage or chopped sage. Add liver strips to seasoned flour; toss to coat.
2. Heat butter or margarine and oil in a large skillet. Add coated liver; sauté over medium heat 2 minutes. Turn liver; add sage leaves. Cook 2 minutes. With a spatula, remove liver from skillet; discard sage leaves. Set liver aside; keep warm.
3. Add consommé and lemon juice to skillet. Increase heat; bring sauce quickly to a boil, stirring constantly. Season with salt and pepper.
4. Spoon rice into a serving dish; top with cooked liver. Pour sauce over liver. Garnish with sage sprigs. Makes 4 servings.

Clockwise from top left: Liver with Fresh Sage, Turkey in Sweet & Sour Sauce, Ham Steaks with Cucumber Sauce

Steak with Anchovies

1 (1-1/2-lb.) beef-loin top sirloin steak
Freshly ground pepper
3 tablespoons butter or margarine, room temperature
1 tablespoon vegetable oil
1 tablespoon chopped fresh parsley
2 drops lemon juice
1 (2-oz.) can anchovy fillets, drained

To garnish:
Parsley sprigs
Tomato roses, box, opposite page

Preparation and cooking time: 15 minutes

1. Season steak with pepper.
2. Heat 1 tablespoon butter or margarine and oil in a large skillet over medium-high heat. Add steak; cook 2 minutes. Turn steak. Cook 2 minutes.
3. Reduce heat to medium; cook 1 to 3 minutes on each side or until steak is cooked to desired doneness.
4. While meat is cooking, in a small bowl, beat remaining butter or margarine, parsley, lemon juice and pepper until blended. Shape into a roll; freeze a few minutes.
5. To serve, cut steak into serving pieces. Arrange anchovy fillets on steak pieces. Immediately before serving, cut parsley-butter roll into 4 to 6 pieces; place parsley-butter pieces on steak. Garnish with parsley and tomato roses.
6. Serve with cooked spinach blended with sour cream and freshly grated nutmeg. Makes 4 to 6 servings.

Steak with Anchovies

Rarebit with Mushrooms

4 large bread slices
1/4 cup butter or margarine
6 oz. mushrooms, sliced
1 tablespoon chopped fresh parsley
3 tablespoons all-purpose flour
1/2 cup dark ale or cider
2 teaspoons prepared mustard
2 cups shredded sharp Cheddar cheese (8 oz.)
2 eggs, slightly beaten
Salt
Freshly ground black pepper
Pinch of red (cayenne) pepper

Preparation and cooking time: 15 minutes

1. Preheat broiler. Toast bread in a toaster or broiler.
2. Melt 2 tablespoon butter or margarine over low heat. Add mushrooms; sauté 5 minutes. Stir in parsley; set aside.
3. Melt remaining butter or margarine in a medium saucepan over medium heat. Stir in flour; cook 1 minute, stirring constantly. Gradually stir in ale or cider; bring to a boil. Simmer 2 minutes. Remove pan from heat; stir in mustard, cheese and eggs. Season with salt, black pepper and red pepper. Stir until cheese melts.
4. Place toast in a 9-inch-square baking pan. Spoon mushrooms over toast; spoon cheese mixture over mushrooms. Broil under preheated broiler until brown and bubbling. Makes 4 servings.

Variations

This melt-in-the-mouth savory is delicious with other quick-cooking foods, too. Substitute cooked ham slices or cooked shrimp for mushrooms. Or, serve rarebit with broiled bacon and tomatoes or with poached eggs.

Sausage Rolls

8 precooked sausage links
8 bacon slices
16 prunes, pitted
4 pita-bread rounds, split, warmed

Preparation and cooking time: 15 minutes

1. Preheat broiler. Cut each sausage in half crosswise.
2. Stretch bacon slices on a work surface. Cut each slice in half crosswise.
3. Roll each sausage half and a prune in a bacon piece. Thread 4 rolls on a short skewer. Repeat with remaining rolls.
4. Place skewers on a broiler-pan rack. Broil under preheated broiler 5 to 6 minutes or until bacon is crisp, turning once.
5. Remove skewers; divide sausage rolls among pieces of pita. Serve hot. Makes 4 servings.

Tomato Roses

Using a vegetable, peeler, peel firm-skinned tomatoes in a single strip. Peel should have a little flesh on it. Loosely roll the peel as shown, making a rose. Add smooth parsley for leaves. Tomato roses enhance the appearance of cold platters and salads. Use the remaining tomato flesh as platter or salad ingredient.

Left to right: Banana & Rum Flambé, Raspberry Cream, Ginger
Soufflé Omelet, Fruity Yogurt Dessert

Banana & Rum Flambé

3 tablespoons butter or margarine
4 ripe bananas, peeled, halved lengthwise
1/3 cup packed light-brown sugar
2 tablespoons blanched almonds
2 tablespoons rum
To serve:
Whipped cream or ice cream

Preparation and cooking time: 10 minutes

1. Melt butter or margarine in a shallow flameproof dish;
add bananas in 1 layer. Sprinkle with sugar and almonds.
2. Sauté bananas over medium heat 3 minutes; turn. Sauté
until golden brown.
3. In a small saucepan, warm rum. Pour over bananas;
carefully ignite rum. Serve while flaming. Serve with
whipped cream or ice cream. Makes 4 servings.

Raspberry Cream

1/2 pint whipping cream (1 cup)
1/3 cup sugar
1 tablespoon Marsala, if desired
2 egg whites
8 oz. fresh raspberries, or frozen raspberries, thawed
5 macaroons, broken into 4 pieces each

---

*Preparation: 10 minutes, plus thawing if using frozen
raspberries*

1. In a medium bowl, whip cream until stiff peaks form.
Beat in sugar and Marsala, if desired.
2. In a medium bowl, beat egg whites until stiff but not
dry. Fold beaten egg whites into cream mixture.
3. Reserve a few berries to decorate. Just before serving,
stir raspberries and macaroons into cream mixture. Spoon
into 4 sherbet or wine glasses; decorate with reserved
fruit. Makes 4 servings.

Ginger Soufflé Omelet

6 eggs, separated
3 tablespoons granulated sugar
2 tablespoons butter or margarine
2 tablespoons chopped stem ginger preserved in syrup
1/4 cup apricot jam
1 tablespoon powdered sugar, sifted

Preparation and cooking time: 15 minutes

1. In a medium bowl, beat egg yolks and granulated sugar until combined. In a medium bowl, beat egg whites until stiff but not dry. Fold beaten egg whites into egg-yolk mixture.
2. Melt butter or margarine in a large skillet over medium heat. Pour in egg mixture, spreading evenly over skillet bottom. Cook omelet about 3 minutes or until bottom is golden brown.
3. Preheat broiler. Stir stem ginger into jam.
4. Broil omelet under preheated broiler 2 minutes or until firm and golden brown on top. Spread with jam mixture; broil 1 minute.
5. Decorate top with sifted powdered sugar. Cut into wedges; serve immediately. Makes 4 servings.

Fruity Yogurt Dessert

2 egg whites
2 tablespoons light-brown sugar
1 (8-oz.) carton peach or other fruit yogurt
1 large banana, peeled, chopped
1 teaspoon lemon juice
2 tablespoons mixed dried fruit
1 tablespoon chopped mixed candied fruit
2 tablespoons chopped nuts

Preparation time: 10 minutes

1. In a medium bowl, beat egg whites until soft peaks form. Beat in brown sugar until stiff and glossy. Fold in yogurt.
2. In a small bowl, toss banana in lemon juice. Fold banana, dried fruit and candied fruit into yogurt mixture.
3. Spoon mixture into 4 sherbet or wine glasses; sprinkle with nuts.
4. Refrigerate 15 to 30 minutes; this dessert needs to be eaten soon after making. Makes 4 servings.

Melon, Pimento & Ham Salad

Pimento Mayonnaise:
1/2 cup mayonnaise
1 tablespoon dairy sour cream
2 canned pimentos, drained
1 tablespoon tomato paste
Salt
Freshly ground pepper

Salad:
8 oz. cooked ham, diced
4 oz. seedless green grapes
8 to 10 walnut halves
1/2 honeydew or other melon, chilled

To garnish:
Lettuce leaves

Preparation: 30 minutes

1. To prepare mayonnaise, in a blender or food processor fitted with a steel blade, process mayonnaise, sour cream, pimentos, tomato paste, salt and pepper until smooth.
2. In a medium bowl, combine Pimento Mayonnaise with ham, grapes and walnuts.
3. Discard seeds from melon; make melon balls, using a melon baller or teaspoon. Or, peel melon; cut into small cubes.
4. Arrange lettuce leaves in a serving dish. Place ham salad in center of lettuce; surround with a ring of melon balls or cubes. Makes 4 servings.

Variation
Substitute diced cooked chicken for ham. Chicken is excellent combined with Pimento Mayonnaise.

Melon Bowl

For a special presentation, use a melon as a container. It looks especially attractive filled with fruit salad or frosty fruit sherbet decorated with mint sprigs.

To make a melon bowl, cut a slice from top of melon; scoop out and discard seeds. Remove part of melon pulp, leaving a thin wall. Use a teaspoon or a grapefruit knife with a curved blade to remove pulp. Cut zigzag points around top of melon. Use melon pulp as part of salad, if desired. Fill melon with fruit salad or sherbet.

Skillet Pizza

1-1/2 cups self-rising flour
Freshly ground pepper
1/2 teaspoon Italian seasoning
1/4 cup water
1/4 cup olive oil
1/3 cup tomato sauce
2 medium tomatoes, peeled, sliced
1 tablespoon chopped fresh basil or parsley
4 oz. thinly sliced salami
12 pimento-stuffed olives, sliced
4 to 5 slices mozzarella cheese

Preparation: 30 minutes

1. Preheat broiler. In a medium bowl, combine flour, pepper and Italian seasoning. Stir in water and 2 tablespoons olive oil to form a soft dough.
2. On a lightly floured surface, knead dough until smooth. Roll out dough to a 9-inch circle.
3. Heat 1 tablespoon of remaining oil in a large skillet. Add dough circle; cook over medium heat 5 minutes. Remove from skillet. Add remaining 1 tablespoon oil to skillet. Return dough circle to pan; cook on other side 5 minutes.
4. When crust is golden brown on both sides, remove pan from heat. If skillet handle is not flameproof, transfer pizza crust to a baking sheet. Spread crust with tomato sauce; cover with sliced tomatoes. Sprinkle with basil or parsley.
5. Arrange salami slices, slightly overlapping, on tomatoes. Top with sliced olives. Arrange cheese slices in center of pizza.
6. Broil under preheated broiler 5 minutes or until cheese is melted. Cut into wedges; serve hot. Makes 2 servings.

Variation
Seafood Pizza: Cook pizza dough as directed above. Cover with tomato sauce, sliced tomatoes and chopped herbs. Substitute 1 (4-oz.) can drained shrimp and 1 (4-oz.) jar mussels or smoked oysters for salami. Sprinkle with freshly ground black pepper and a pinch of red (cayenne) pepper. Top with olives and cheese. Broil as directed above.

Top to bottom: Skillet Pizza, Melon, Pimento & Ham Salad

Cottage-Cheese Salad & Muffins

Muffins:
2 cups all-purpose flour
2 tablespoons sugar
2-1/2 teaspoons baking powder
1 teaspoon salt
2 eggs
3/4 cup milk
3 tablespoons vegetable oil

Salad:
1 cup cream-style cottage cheese
1/2 pint dairy sour cream (1 cup)
1 cup finely diced radishes, cucumber or green onions
Salt
Freshly ground pepper
Lettuce leaves

Preparation and cooking time: 30 minutes

1. Preheat oven to 400F (205C). Grease a 12-cup muffin pan or line with paper baking cups.
2. In a large bowl, combine flour, sugar, baking powder and salt.
3. Beat eggs in a small bowl. Beat in milk and oil until well blended. Pour milk mixture into flour mixture; stir until flour is moistened. Batter will be lumpy. Spoon batter into prepared muffin cups.
4. Bake in preheated oven 20 to 25 minutes or until lightly browned. Remove muffins from pan immediately.
5. Prepare salad while muffins are baking. In a medium bowl, combine cottage cheese and sour cream. Stir in vegetables, salt and pepper.
6. Line individual serving dishes with lettuce. Spoon cottage-cheese mixture over lettuce; serve with hot muffins. Makes 4 servings.

Variations
Whole-Wheat Muffins: Substitute 1 cup all-purpose flour and 3/4 cup whole-wheat flour for all-purpose flour. Increase sugar to 1/4 cup and baking powder to 1 tablespoon.
Herbed Muffins: Add 2 teaspoons Italian seasoning and 1/4 teaspoon dry mustard to dry ingredients.

Scrambled Eggs with Peppers

1 green bell pepper, halved
6 bread slices
8 eggs
2 teaspoons prepared mustard
Salt
Freshly ground pepper
1 tablespoon butter or margarine
1/2 (8-oz.) pkg. cream cheese, room temperature
2 tablespoons whipping cream

Preparation and cooking time: 20 minutes

1. Preheat broiler. Place pepper, cut-side down, on a broiler-pan rack. Broil under preheated broiler 4 to 5 minutes or until skin turns black and blisters. Cool broiled pepper; peel off skin. Cut peeled pepper lengthwise into thin strips.
2. Toast bread under broiler or in a toaster. Cut each slice into 4 triangles. Remove crusts, if desired.
3. In a medium bowl, beat eggs and mustard. Season with salt and pepper.
4. Melt butter or margarine in a large skillet over medium heat. Add egg mixture; stir 3 to 4 minutes or until eggs begin to set.
5. Stir in cheese; cook about 2 minutes or until mixture is softly set. Stir in cream.
6. Spoon egg mixture into a serving dish; arrange toast around edge. Crisscross pepper strips over top. Serve immediately. Makes 4 servings.

Stir-Fried Chicken

4 chicken-breast halves, boneless
2 tablespoons cornstarch
3 tablespoons soy sauce
5 tablespoons vegetable oil
2 garlic cloves, finely chopped
4 green bell peppers, sliced
3 tablespoons blanched almonds
Salt
Freshly ground black pepper

Preparation and cooking time: 25 minutes

1. Cut chicken into small cubes. In a medium bowl, combine chicken cubes and cornstarch. Stir in 2 tablespoons soy sauce and 2 tablespoons oil.
2. In a large skillet, heat remaining oil. Add garlic, bell peppers and almonds. Stir-fry 3 minutes. Remove with a slotted spoon; keep warm.
3. Drain chicken; add to oil remaining in skillet. Stir-fry 4 to 5 minutes or until chicken is done.
4. Return bell-pepper mixture to skillet; stir in remaining soy sauce. Season with black pepper.
5. Serve hot over hot cooked noodles or rice. Makes 4 servings.

Top to bottom: Scrambled Eggs with Peppers, Stir-Fried Chicken

Pork in Orange & Ginger Sauce

2 pork-loin tenderloins, about 1-1/2 lb. total weight
4 teaspoons all-purpose flour
Salt
Freshly ground pepper
1/4 teaspoon dried leaf thyme
2 tablespoons butter or margarine
2 oranges
2 tablespoons ginger-flavored brandy
1 teaspoon grated fresh gingerroot
1/4 cup whipping cream

Preparation and cooking time: 30 minutes

1. Cut pork into 1-inch slices. In a plastic bag, combine flour, salt, pepper and thyme.
2. Melt butter or margarine in a large skillet. Add pork; sauté over medium-high heat 2 minutes per side. Reduce heat to medium; cover pan with lid or foil. Cook 10 minutes, turning once.
3. Grate peel and squeeze juice from 1 orange. Cut remaining orange into 8 wedges for garnish.
4. With tongs, place pork on a serving dish; keep warm. Add 2 tablespoons orange juice and orange peel to skillet; stir in brandy and gingerroot. Season mixture with salt and pepper. Stir in cream; heat until hot. Do not boil.
5. Pour sauce over pork; garnish with orange wedges. Serve with hot cooked rice and a green salad. Makes 4 servings.

Oranges and Lemons

To extract the last drop of juice from an orange or lemon, place fruit on a table. Using flat palm of your hand, roll it firmly backwards and forwards a few times. This releases juice and ensures that none is wasted. Let fruit reach room temperature before squeezing.

Marinated Pork Chops

4 pork chops
2/3 cup beer or apple juice
3 medium onions, sliced
1 bay leaf
6 peppercorns
1 tablespoon molasses
1 tablespoon lemon juice
Freshly ground pepper
2 tablespoons vegetable oil

Preparation and cooking time: 25 minutes, plus at least 2 hours marinating time

1. Place chops, beer or apple juice, 1 sliced onion, bay leaf and peppercorns in a shallow dish. Cover and refrigerate at least 2 hours.
2. Preheat broiler. Remove chops from marinade; strain sauce into a medium saucepan. Bring sauce to a boil; boil 4 minutes or until mixture is reduced by 1/2.
3. Stir in molasses, lemon juice and pepper.
4. Brush 1 side of chops with sauce; broil under preheated broiler 4 to 5 minutes. Turn chops; brush other side with sauce. Broil 4 to 5 minutes or until pork is no longer pink.
5. Heat oil in a medium skillet over medium heat. Add remaining onions; sauté 2 minutes. Add remaining sauce; simmer 5 minutes.
6. To serve, spoon glazed onions over broiled chops. Makes 4 servings.

Marinating

Here's a simple way to marinate meat and fish. Place meat or fish into a heavy plastic bag. Be sure to check bag for holes before using. Add marinade. Seal bag with a twist tie. Turn bag occasionally to distribute marinade. This method works well for marinating a piece of meat that is large or odd shaped, or for cubes of meat or fish that need to be turned frequently.

Crispy-Coated Liver

6 tablespoons butter or margarine
1 large onion, sliced into rings
1/4 cup all-purpose flour
Salt
Freshly ground pepper
1/2 teaspoon Italian seasoning
1 egg
1 tablespoon milk
1 lb. calves' liver, thinly sliced diagonally
3/4 cup regular rolled oats
1/2 cup medium sherry
1/2 cup chicken stock

To garnish:
Parsley sprigs

Preparation and cooking time: 25 minutes

1. Melt 2 tablespoons butter or margarine in a large skillet over medium heat. Add onion; sauté 5 to 6 minutes, turning occasionally. Remove onion from skillet; keep warm.
2. In a shallow bowl, combine flour, salt, pepper and Italian seasoning. In a shallow bowl, beat egg and milk until combined. Pat liver dry with paper towels. Dip liver first into seasoned flour until coated on both sides, then dip into egg mixture. Finally, coat with oats, pressing in oats to coat evenly.
3. Melt remaining butter or margarine in skillet used for onions. Add coated liver; sauté over medium heat 3 minutes per side or until coating is crisp and brown. Liver should be slightly pink inside; pierce with point of a sharp knife to test.
4. Remove liver from pan with tongs; keep warm. Stir any remaining seasoned flour into fat remaining in skillet. Stir 1 minute. Gradually stir in sherry and stock; bring to a boil. Season with salt and pepper.
5. Arrange liver in a heated serving dish; scatter cooked onion over liver. Spoon sauce over liver and onion. Garnish with parsley. Makes 4 servings.

Crispy-Coated Liver

Sole in Sweet & Sour Sauce

4 sole fillets, about 6 oz. each
4 oz. mushrooms, sliced
1 red bell pepper, thinly sliced
2 tablespoons sliced blanched almonds
Sauce:
1 tablespoon cornstarch
1/4 cup orange juice
Grated peel of 1 orange
1 tablespoon light-brown sugar
1 tablespoon honey
1 tablespoon cider vinegar
1 tablespoon tomato paste
1 tablespoon soy sauce
1 tablespoon sweet sherry
1 tablespoon vegetable oil
1 teaspoon hot-pepper sauce
Salt
Freshly ground pepper

To garnish:
Lemon slices
Parsley sprigs

Preparation and cooking time: 20 minutes

1. Cut 4 (12" x 8") foil pieces; brush centers with a little oil. Trim fish; arrange each fillet on an oiled foil piece. Scatter mushrooms, bell pepper and almonds over fish. Bring up sides of foil to make a dish shape.
2. To prepare sauce, in a medium bowl, combine cornstarch and orange juice. Stir in remaining sauce ingredients.
3. Pour sauce over fish. Fold and seal edges of foil firmly to make watertight packages. Place in a steamer or colander over boiling water; steam 20 minutes.
4. Serve fish in foil parcels, if desired. Or, carefully remove from package; place on individual plates. Garnish with lemon and parsley.
5. Serve with hot cooked rice or noodles. Makes 4 servings.

Chicken Cutlets with Vegetable Kabobs

6 tablespoons butter or margarine, room temperature
1 teaspoon paprika
1 teaspoon tomato paste
1/4 teaspoon Worcestershire sauce
Salt
Freshly ground black pepper
4 chicken cutlets
3 tablespoons vegetable oil
1 tablespoon red-wine vinegar
4 small zucchini, cut into 3/4-inch slices
4 oz. small mushrooms
1 red or yellow bell pepper, cut into 1-1/4-inch squares

Preparation and cooking time: 30 minutes

1. In a small bowl, beat butter or margarine, paprika, tomato paste, Worcestershire sauce, salt and black pepper until combined.
2. Spread 1/2 of mixture on both sides of cutlets. Shape remaining butter or margarine mixture into 8 pats; refrigerate.
3. Preheat broiler. In a small bowl, combine oil and vinegar; season with salt and black pepper. Add zucchini, mushrooms and bell pepper; toss to coat. Drain vegetables; thread on 4 small skewers.
4. Place chicken breasts on a broiler-pan rack. Broil under preheated broiler 15 minutes. Turn chicken; place kabobs on rack with chicken. Broil 6 minutes, turning kabobs once. Baste kabobs with remaining oil-and-vinegar mixture.
5. Serve hot with 2 chilled butter pats on each chicken piece. Makes 4 servings.

Trout with Apples

4 large rainbow trout, ready to cook
Freshly ground pepper
1 tablespoon lemon juice
4 fresh rosemary sprigs or 2 teaspoons dried rosemary
1/4 cup butter or margarine
2 apples, cored, thickly sliced

To garnish:
1 lemon, quartered

Preparation and cooking time: 25 minutes

1. Sprinkle inside each trout with pepper and lemon juice; place a rosemary sprig inside each trout. Or, sprinkle inside each trout with 1/2 of dried rosemary.
2. Melt butter or margarine in a large skillet over medium heat. Add trout; cook 6 minutes. Using spatulas, turn fish, taking care not to break skin. Add apples. Cook 6 to 8 minutes or until fish tests done and apples are golden brown, turning apples once. Transfer to a warm serving dish.
3. Serve fish surrounded by apples; garnish with lemon wedges. Makes 4 servings.

Sole in Sweet & Sour Sauce, Cooked spaghetti

Peach Caramels

4 large ripe peaches, peeled, halved
2 teaspoons lemon juice
1 tablespoon ground almonds
2 to 3 drops almond extract
1 tablespoon sugar
3/4 cup whipping cream, whipped
2 tablespoons chopped blanched almonds, toasted

Sauce:
2/3 cup packed light-brown sugar
2 tablespoons butter or margarine
1 tablespoon milk

Preparation and cooking time: 20 minutes

1. In a medium bowl, toss peaches in lemon juice. Stir ground almonds, almond extract and sugar into whipped cream.
2. Fill peach cavities with almond cream, reserving a little for decoration. Sandwich peach halves together; arrange on a serving dish.
3. To prepare sauce, in a medium saucepan, combine brown sugar, butter or margarine and milk. Bring to a boil; simmer over low heat 7 minutes. Remove from heat; beat with a wooden spoon 1 minute or until sauce is smooth.
4. Slowly spoon sauce over peaches; do not cover completely.
5. When sauce has cooled, spoon or pipe remaining cream on peaches; top with toasted almonds. Makes 4 servings.

Poached Pears with Chocolate Sauce

1-1/2 cups water
1/2 cup sugar
1/4 teaspoon vanilla extract
4 large ripe pears, peeled
4 oz. semisweet chocolate

Preparation and cooking time: 20 to 25 minutes

1. In a medium saucepan, combine water, sugar and vanilla; bring to a boil.
2. Add pears; poach pears over medium heat 10 minutes or until tender, turning occasionally. With a slotted spoon, carefully remove pears from poaching liquid; keep warm.
3. Break chocolate into pieces; add to poaching liquid. Stir until melted. Beat until smooth; simmer 10 minutes or until sauce is thick enough to coat a spoon.
4. Serve pears warm; serve sauce separately.
5. Or, refrigerate pears until chilled. Serve with hot or cold chocolate sauce and whipped cream. Makes 4 servings.

Drop Scones with Blueberry Sauce

Scones:
3/4 cup all-purpose flour
2 teaspoons baking powder
Pinch of salt
1 egg, beaten
1/2 cup milk
Vegetable oil for cooking
2/3 cup dairy sour cream

Blueberry Sauce:
1 cup fresh or frozen blueberries
2 tablespoons blueberry jam or blackberry jam
1 teaspoon lemon juice
1 tablespoon sugar, if necessary

Preparation and cooking time: 30 minutes

1. Sift flour, baking powder and salt into a medium bowl. Stir in egg; gradually beat in milk. Beat until batter is smooth.
2. Lightly grease a heavy skillet with vegetable oil; place over medium heat. Drop batter, 1 tablespoon at a time, into hot skillet. Leave 2 to 3 inches between scones to allow spreading.
3. Cook over medium heat 2 to 3 minutes or until bubbles appear on surface. Turn; cook 2 to 3 minutes or until golden brown. Repeat with remaining batter. Keep warm.
4. To prepare sauce, combine blueberries, jam and lemon juice in a medium saucepan. Bring to a boil. Simmer 2 minutes. Add sugar, if necessary.
5. Place warm scones on a serving plate. Serve with sauce and sour cream separately. Makes 12 to 16 scones.

Clockwise from top left: Peach Caramels, Poached Pear with Chocolate Sauce, Drop Scones with Blueberry Sauce

In Forty-Five Minutes

Broiled Chicken with Cheese

4 chicken-breast halves, boneless
1/4 cup vegetable oil
1 tablespoon lemon juice
1 teaspoon dried leaf thyme
Salt
Freshly ground pepper
4 oz. cooked ham, thinly sliced
2 oz. Swiss cheese, thinly sliced
2 large tomatoes, sliced

Preparation and cooking time: 45 minutes

1. Preheat broiler. Cut 4 (12-inch-square) foil pieces.
2. With a sharp knife, cut 3 slits in each chicken breast. Lay on foil.
3. In a small bowl, combine oil, lemon juice, thyme, salt and pepper.
4. Draw foil up around chicken. Pour oil mixture over chicken; carefully seal packages.
5. Cook chicken packages under preheated broiler, turning once, 35 minutes or until juices run clear when chicken is pierced with a skewer.
6. Carefully open packages; arrange ham, cheese and finally tomatoes on chicken breasts. Spoon cooking juices over tomatoes. Broil 3 to 4 minutes or until cheese is bubbling.
7. Serve with hot corn-on-the-cob, if desired. Makes 4 servings.

Veal & Mushroom Rolls

4 veal cutlets, about 3 oz. each
6 tablespoons butter or margarine
2 oz. mushrooms, finely chopped
2 tablespoons raisins
1 tablespoon chopped fresh parsley
2 tablespoons shredded Cheddar cheese
Salt
Freshly ground pepper
2 teaspoons all-purpose flour
3/4 cup red wine

To garnish:
Parsley sprigs

Preparation and cooking time: 45 minutes

1. Pound cutlets with a meat mallet or rolling pin until flattened. Cut each cutlet in half.
2. Melt 2 tablespoons butter or margarine in a medium skillet. Add mushrooms; sauté 2 minutes. Cool slightly; stir in raisins, parsley, cheese, salt and pepper.
3. Divide filling among veal pieces; press firmly. Roll up veal; tie with kitchen string.
4. Melt remaining butter or margarine in a large skillet over medium heat. Add veal rolls; sauté about 8 minutes or until evenly browned, turning occasionally.
5. Remove veal rolls from skillet with tongs; keep warm. Stir flour into fat remaining in skillet; cook 1 minute. Gradually stir in wine; bring to a boil. Season with salt and pepper. Return veal rolls to skillet. Cover; simmer 10 minutes, turning once.
6. To serve, remove strings; garnish with parsley. Makes 4 servings.

Top to bottom: Broiled Chicken with Cheese, Veal & Mushroom Rolls

Left to right: Carrot & Corn Casserole, Bacon & Corn Chowder

Carrot & Corn Casserole

1 lb. carrots, sliced
1 tablespoon butter or margarine
2 teaspoons honey
3 tablespoons chicken stock
Salt
Freshly ground pepper
1 (12-oz.) can whole-kernel corn, drained
1 tablespoon chopped fresh parsley

Topping:
3/4 cup whole-wheat flour
1/2 teaspoon salt
5 tablespoons butter or margarine
1/2 cup fresh bread crumbs
Pinch of ground ginger

Preparation and cooking time: 40 minutes

1. Preheat oven to 375F (190C). Grease a 1-1/2-quart casserole.
2. Place carrots in a medium saucepan; add enough water to almost cover. Cook over medium heat 10 minutes or until crisp-tender. Drain carrots; stir in butter or margarine, honey, chicken stock, salt and pepper.
3. Spread carrot mixture in greased casserole. Cover with corn; sprinkle with parsley.
4. To prepare topping, in a small bowl, combine flour and salt. With a pastry blender or 2 knives, cut in butter or margarine until mixture resembles coarse crumbs. Stir in bread crumbs and ginger. Sprinkle topping over vegetables.
5. Bake in preheated oven 20 minutes or until topping is crisp and brown. Serve hot. Makes 4 servings.

Bacon & Corn Chowder

4 bacon slices, diced
1 medium onion, sliced
1 medium leek, sliced
2 celery stalks, sliced
2 medium carrots, thinly sliced
1 cup chicken stock
1-1/2 cups diced potatoes
1 (12-oz.) can whole-kernel corn, drained
1-1/2 cups milk
Salt
Freshly ground black pepper
Pinch of red (cayenne) pepper
6 tablespoons whipping cream

To garnish:
1 tablespoon chopped fresh parsley

Preparation and cooking time: 45 minutes

1. Sauté bacon in a medium saucepan over medium heat 3 minutes or until browned.
2. Stir in onion, leek, celery and carrots; cook 4 minutes.
3. Add stock; bring to a boil. Add potatoes; return to a boil. Cover pan; simmer 20 minutes.
4. Add corn and milk; heat to the simmering point. Simmer 3 minutes; season with salt, black pepper and red pepper.
5. Stir in cream; heat until hot.
6. Garnish with parsley. Serve hot with hot crusty rolls. Makes 4 servings.

Cheese & Olive Puffs

2 cups shredded sharp Cheddar cheese (8 oz.)
2 eggs, separated
2 tablespoons beer
1/4 teaspoon salt
Freshly ground pepper
1/3 cup all-purpose flour
1 teaspoon baking powder
24 pimento-stuffed olives
Vegetable oil for deep-frying

Salad:
2 medium, firm tomatoes, sliced
2 green onions, sliced
1 tablespoon freshly chopped basil
5 tablespoons prepared French dressing

Preparation and cooking time: 30 minutes, plus 30 minutes standing.

1. In a medium bowl, beat cheese, egg yolks and beer until blended. Add salt and pepper.
2. Sift flour and baking powder; stir into cheese mixture.
3. In a medium bowl, beat egg whites until stiff but not dry; fold beaten egg whites into cheese mixture. Cover bowl; let stand 30 minutes.
4. To prepare salad, arrange tomato slices around edge of a serving plate; sprinkle with onions and basil. Pour French dressing over salad. Refrigerate until served.
5. Dust hands with flour; shape cheese mixture into 24 walnut-sized balls. Gently push 1 olive into center of each ball. Shape cheese mixture around olive until completely enclosed.
6. Heat oil to 375F (190C) in a deep saucepan or deep-fryer. Deep-fry, a few at a time, 2 to 3 minutes or until puffed and golden. Drain on paper towels. Repeat with remaining balls. Place balls in a small bowl; place bowl in center of salad. Serve immediately. Makes 4 servings of 6 puffs each.

Cheese & Olive Puffs

Mixed-Vegetable Curry

1 small cauliflower, cut into flowerets
1-1/3 cups diced carrots
1-1/4 cups diced potatoes
Water
1-1/2 cups green peas
3 tablespoon butter or margarine
1 large onion, sliced
1 tablespoon curry powder
1 tablespoon all-purpose flour
Salt
2 tablespoons mango chutney
Water or chicken stock
2/3 cup half and half
2 tablespoons blanched almonds

To garnish:
4 hard-cooked eggs, cut into wedges
Pinch of paprika

Preparation and cooking time: 40 minutes

1. Steam cauliflower, carrots and potatoes over boiling water 6 minutes or until crisp-tender. Bring 1 cup water to a boil in a medium saucepan; add peas. Cook peas 5 minutes.
2. Drain vegetables, reserving cooking liquid from peas. Keep cooked vegetables warm.
3. Melt butter or margarine in a large saucepan. Add onion; sauté over low heat 5 minutes. Stir in curry powder, flour and salt; cook 1 minute. Stir in chutney.
4. Pour cooking liquid into a 2-cup measuring cup; add enough water or chicken stock to make 2 cups. Gradually stir into curry mixture; bring to a boil. Simmer 5 minutes; stir in half and half.
5. Stir in vegetables; heat until hot. Stir in almonds.
6. Serve hot; garnish with egg wedges and paprika. Serve with hot cooked rice. Makes 4 servings.

Blue-Cheese Soufflé

Parmesan cheese or seasoned dry bread crumbs
2-1/2 tablespoons butter or margarine
3 tablespoons all-purpose flour
1 cup milk
Red (cayenne) pepper
Salt
Freshly ground black pepper
1 cup crumbled blue cheese or Roquefort cheese (4 oz.)
4 egg yolks
5 egg whites

Preparation and cooking time: 45 minutes

1. Preheat oven to 375F (190C). Heavily grease a 6-cup soufflé dish; sprinkle bottom and side with Parmesan cheese or bread crumbs. Shake out excess cheese or crumbs.
2. Melt butter or margarine in a medium saucepan. Stir in flour; cook over low heat 2 minutes. Gradually stir in milk; cook until thickened, stirring constantly. Stir in red pepper, salt and black pepper.
3. Stir in cheese. Cook over low heat 1 to 2 minutes or until cheese is melted.
4. Remove saucepan from heat; beat in egg yolks, 1 at a time, beating well after each addition.
5. Beat egg whites until stiff but not dry. Stir 2 tablespoons beaten egg whites into sauce. Fold in remaining egg whites. Spoon mixture into prepared soufflé dish.
6. Bake in preheated oven 30 to 35 minutes or until soufflé is firm and golden on top.
7. Serve immediately with sliced tomatoes and a tossed green salad. Makes 4 servings.

Cooking Vegetables

Vegetables can be steamed or cooked in boiling water. Steaming has several advantages over cooking vegetables in boiling water. Fewer nutrients are lost in the cooking water; vegetables also have a better texture, color and flavor. Steaming is a good method to use when, as in the recipe for *Mixed-Vegetable Curry*, several vegetables are cooked at once. If the vegetables have different cooking times, add the shorter-cooking ones last.

Always have the water in the steamer or saucepan boiling before adding the vegetables. Leaving the lid off for a few minutes will make green vegetables brighter in color. Vegetable cooking liquid can be used for soup or sauce.

Buy an inexpensive collapsible steamer that fits any saucepan, or improvise with a colander or strainer and a large pan.

Salami & Pasta Salad

Salami & Pasta Salad

1 cup whole-wheat macaroni
Salt
8 oz. new potatoes, scrubbed
1/4 cup prepared French dressing
3 green onions, sliced
1/4 cup walnut halves
1 tablespoon chopped chives
4 oz. salami, diced
4 oz. Swiss cheese, cubed, if desired
6 tablespoons dairy sour cream
1 teaspoon prepared mustard
Freshly ground pepper

Preparation and cooking time: 45 minutes, including cooling

1. Cook macaroni in boiling, salted water according to package directions until tender. Do not overcook. Drain well.
2. At same time, in another saucepan, cook potatoes in boiling, salted water 12 to 15 minutes or until tender. Do not overcook.
3. Drain potatoes; cool until they can be handled. Peel; cut into cubes.
4. While pasta and potatoes are still warm, in a medium bowl, combine with French dressing. Set aside to cool.
5. When pasta and potatoes are cool, stir in green onions; walnuts, reserving a few for garnish; chives; salami; and cheese, if desired.
6. In a small bowl, combine sour cream, mustard and pepper. Stir dressing into salad.
7. Arrange salad in a serving bowl; garnish with reserved walnuts.
8. Serve with chilled melon slices or cubes for a delightful contrast. Makes 4 servings.

Marinated Sirloin Steak

1-1/2 lb. beef sirloin steak
1 medium onion, thinly sliced
1 garlic clove, crushed
2 tablespoons olive oil
1 tablespoon tomato paste
1 tablespoon soy sauce
1 teaspoon hot-pepper sauce
1 tablespoon dark-brown sugar
2 tablespoons thawed frozen orange-juice concentrate
Salt
1 (16-oz.) can tomatoes
1 tablespoon butter or margarine
4 oz. mushrooms, thinly sliced

To garnish:
1 tablespoon chopped fresh parsley

Preparation and cooking time: 45 minutes, plus extra marinating, if possible

1. Cut steak into 4 portions; remove any excess fat.
2. In a glass or stainless-steel bowl, combine onion, garlic, olive oil, tomato paste, soy sauce, hot-pepper sauce, sugar, orange juice and salt. Add steak pieces; turn to coat thoroughly. Let marinate a few minutes or a few hours, as time permits.
3. Place tomatoes in a large saucepan; add steak and marinade. Simmer, uncovered, over medium heat 20 to 25 minutes or until steak is tender and sauce has thickened. Spoon steak and sauce into a warm serving dish.
4. Melt butter or margarine in a small skillet over medium heat. Add mushrooms; sauté 3 to 4 minutes. Spoon over steak mixture. Garnish with parsley.
5. This is a hearty dish, full of flavor. Serve with boiled potatoes and a green vegetable, such as cabbage, lightly simmered in chicken stock and flavored with sesame or caraway seeds. Makes 4 servings.

Variation
When time is not as important, substitute a less-tender cut of meat for the steak. Substitute beef stew cubes or round steak. Cook 1-1/2 to 2 hours. Flavor is even better and meat is more tender if meat is marinated several hours before cooking. This makes a great informal party dish.

Prune-Stuffed Pork Tenderloin

2 pork-loin tenderloins, about 1-1/2 lb. total weight
8 pitted prunes, halved
2 tablespoons raisins
1 tablespoon honey
1 tablespoon butter or margarine
1 teaspoon all-purpose flour
1 cup cider or apple juice
Salt
Freshly ground pepper

Preparation and cooking time: 45 minutes

1. Trim pork; cut each tenderloin lengthwise without cutting completely through.
2. Arrange prune halves along 1 side of each tenderloin. Cover prunes with 1 tablespoon raisins and honey. Close tenderloins over fruit. Secure with wooden picks or tie with kitchen string.
3. Melt butter or margarine in a medium skillet. Add stuffed tenderloins; sauté until brown. Remove from skillet; set aside.
4. Stir flour into fat remaining in skillet; cook 1 minute. Gradually stir in cider or apple juice; bring to a boil.
5. Season with salt and pepper; add remaining raisins. Return tenderloins to skillet. Cover with a lid or foil; simmer 30 minutes, turning once.
6. Serve with hot cooked rice and a green salad. Makes 4 servings.

1/Cut each tenderloin lengthwise without cutting completely through.

2/Cover prunes with 1 tablespoon raisins and honey.

3/Close tenderloins over fruit.

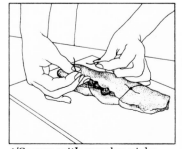
4/Secure with wooden picks or tie with kitchen string.

Chicken Cutlets on Spinach

6 chicken cutlets
2 tablespoons vegetable oil
3 tablespoons butter or margarine
2 lb. fresh spinach
2/3 cup dairy sour cream
1 teaspoon lemon juice
Salt
Freshly ground pepper
To garnish:
1 lemon, quartered

Preparation and cooking time: 45 minutes

1. Roll each chicken cutlet; tie with kitchen string.
2. Heat oil and 1 tablespoon butter or margarine in a large skillet over medium-high heat. Add rolled cutlets; sauté 4 minutes, turning to brown evenly.
3. Reduce heat to low; cook about 10 minutes or until chicken is tender and golden brown.
4. While chicken is cooking, wash spinach; remove tough stems. Place washed spinach in a medium saucepan over medium heat. Cook spinach in water clinging to leaves 8 minutes or until tender.
5. Stir remaining butter or margarine, sour cream and lemon juice into cooked spinach. Season with salt and pepper. Stir over medium heat until spinach and cream makes a smooth thick puree.
6. Spoon spinach mixture into a serving dish; arrange cooked chicken rolls on spinach mixture. Garnish with lemon wedges.
7. Serve with boiled new potatoes. Makes 4 servings.

Prune-Stuffed Pork Tenderloin

Left to right: Pear & Ginger Sponge, Peaches in Marmalade
Sauce, Fruit Bake

Honey Cream

3 eggs, separated
3 tablespoons honey
1/2 pint whipping cream (1 cup)
2 tablespoons medium sherry
2 tablespoons chopped nuts

Preparation and cooking time: 45 minutes, including cooling

1. Combine egg yolks and honey in a medium heatproof bowl. Beat over a pan of hot water 5 minutes or until mixture is light and foamy. Remove bowl from pan; place in a larger bowl of cold water. Stir 2 minutes.
2. In a small bowl, whip cream until stiff peaks form. In a medium bowl, beat egg whites until stiff but not dry.
3. When egg-yolk mixture is cool, stir in sherry. Fold in whipped cream. Fold in beaten egg whites.
4. Spoon mixture into 4 sherbet or wine glasses; sprinkle with nuts. Refrigerate 20 to 30 minutes or until chilled. Makes 4 servings.

Peaches in Marmalade Sauce

4 large ripe peaches, halved
1/4 cup orange marmalade
3 tablespoons butter or margarine
1/4 teaspoon ground cinnamon
2 tablespoons blanched almonds

To serve:
Whipped cream

Preparation and cooking time: 45 minutes

1. Preheat oven to 350F (175C). Arrange peach halves, cut-side up, in a shallow baking dish.
2. In a small saucepan, combine marmalade, butter or margarine and cinnamon. Stir over low heat until marmalade melts; pour over peaches. Sprinkle with nuts. Cover with foil.
3. Bake in preheated oven 35 minutes. Serve hot with whipped cream. Makes 4 servings.

Variation
Substitute canned peach halves for fresh peaches. Drain canned peaches well before using.

Fruit Bake

3 tart apples (about 1 lb.), peeled, thinly sliced
1/4 cup packed light-brown sugar
2 tablespoons orange juice
1/4 cup diced pitted dates
2 firm bananas, thickly sliced
1 teaspoon lemon juice

Topping:
1-1/2 cups all-purpose flour
1/4 teaspoon ground ginger
2 teaspoons baking powder
2 tablespoons butter or margarine
2/3 cup milk
Grated peel of 1 orange
1 teaspoon orange juice
Milk for brushing

Preparation and cooking time: 45 minutes

1. Preheat oven to 425F (220C). Place apples in a 1-quart casserole. Sprinkle with sugar. Pour orange juice over apples. Stir in dates.
2. Sprinkle bananas with lemon juice; place on top of apple mixture.
3. To prepare topping, sift flour, ginger and baking powder into a medium bowl. With a pastry blender or 2 knives, cut in butter or margarine until mixture resembles coarse crumbs.
4. Combine milk, orange peel and orange juice in a small bowl; stir into flour mixture until blended. Knead dough in bowl 10 strokes or until smooth.
5. On a lightly floured surface, roll out dough to 1/2 inch thick. Cut dough into 8 to 10 rounds with a floured round 2-inch cutter.
6. Arrange rounds over fruit. Brush tops with milk.
7. Bake in preheated oven 25 minutes or until topping is golden brown. Serve hot. Makes 4 servings.

Pear & Ginger Sponge

1 lb. very firm pears, peeled, sliced
1/4 cup packed light-brown sugar
1/2 teaspoon ground ginger
2 pieces stem ginger preserved in syrup, thinly sliced

Sponge Topping:
1/4 cup butter or margarine, room temperature
1 cup all-purpose flour, sifted
1/4 cup packed light-brown sugar
1-1/2 teaspoons baking powder
1 teaspoon ground ginger
1 egg, beaten
1/3 cup milk

To serve:
Vanilla custard sauce or sweetened whipped cream

Preparation and cooking time: 45 minutes

1. Preheat oven to 400F (205C). Grease an 8-inch cake pan or 1-1/2-quart baking dish. Arrange pear slices in bottom of greased pan or dish. Combine sugar, ground ginger and stem ginger in a small bowl; sprinkle over pears.
2. To prepare sponge, beat butter or margarine, flour, sugar, baking powder, ginger, egg and milk in a large bowl at low speed until blended. Increase speed to high; beat 2 minutes. Spread batter evenly over pears.
3. Bake in preheated oven 30 minutes or until cake tester inserted in center of cake comes out clean. Serve hot with custard sauce or sweetened whipped cream. Makes 4 servings.

Brown Rice with Crisp Vegetables

2 tablespoons olive oil
1 medium onion, sliced
1 garlic clove, crushed
1-1/2 cups uncooked long-grain brown rice
3-3/4 cups hot chicken stock
Salt
Freshly ground pepper
1 small cauliflower, cut into small flowerets
2 cups diced carrots
2 leeks, sliced
1 cup green peas
2 tablespoons butter or margarine
1 cup shredded Cheddar cheese (4 oz.)
1 tablespoon chopped fresh mint
1 tablespoon chopped fresh parsley

To serve:
Grated Parmesan cheese

Preparation and cooking time: 1 hour

1. Heat olive oil over medium heat in a medium saucepan. Add onion and garlic; sauté 2 minutes, stirring once or twice. Stir in rice; cook 1 minute.
2. Stir in stock, salt and pepper; bring to a boil. Cover pan; reduce heat. Simmer 40 minutes. Rice should be tender and all stock absorbed.
3. While rice is cooking, steam cauliflower, carrots, leeks and peas 6 to 8 minutes or until crisp-tender. Do not overcook.
4. Melt butter or margarine in a large skillet. Add steamed vegetables; sauté, stirring frequently, about 4 minutes or until glazed but not brown.
5. Stir glazed vegetables, Cheddar cheese and mint into cooked rice. Garnish with parsley; serve immediately. Serve Parmesan cheese separately.
6. Serve with French bread spread with garlic butter, wrapped in foil and then baked in a 350F (175C) oven 15 minutes. Makes 4 servings.

Variation
White Rice with Crisp Vegetables: Substitute long-grain white rice for brown rice. Reduce chicken stock to 3 cups. Cook about 20 minutes.

Lentil & Watercress Patties

3 tablespoons vegetable oil
1 large onion, finely chopped
1 garlic clove, crushed
1 cup plus 2 tablespoons lentils (8 oz.), washed, drained
2 cups chicken stock
Few parsley sprigs
2 tablespoons tomato paste
1 cup chopped blanched almonds
1 bunch watercress, finely chopped
1 tablespoon chopped fresh mint
Salt
Freshly ground pepper
2 tablespoons all-purpose flour
Vegetable oil for frying

Preparation and cooking time: 1 hour

1. Heat 3 tablespoons oil in a medium saucepan over medium heat. Add onion and garlic; sauté 2 minutes, stirring once or twice. Stir in lentils until coated with oil.
2. Stir in stock and parsley; bring to a boil. Reduce heat; cover saucepan. Simmer 40 minutes or until lentils are soft and stock is completely absorbed. Remove from heat; discard parsley.
3. Beat lentils with a wooden spoon until blended; beat in tomato paste, almonds, watercress and mint. Season with salt and pepper.
4. Shape mixture into 12 flat patties. Coat with flour.
5. Heat oil in a large skillet over medium heat. Add enough patties to fill skillet; sauté about 5 minutes per side or until crisp. Drain on paper towels. Repeat with remaining patties. Serve hot or cold.
6. Serve hot patties with creamy mashed potatoes and a green vegetable. Serve cold patties with a salad for an unusual picnic snack. Makes 4 servings.

Top to bottom: White Rice with Crisp Vegetables, Lentil & Watercress Patties

Shrimp Mille-Feuille

1/2 (17-1/2-oz) pkg. puff pastry, thawed, if frozen

Filling:
6 tablespoons butter or margarine, room temperature
1/4 cup all-purpose flour
1 cup milk
8 oz. shrimp, cooked, peeled, deveined
1 teaspoon lemon juice
Few drops of hot-pepper sauce
Salt
Freshly ground white pepper
Pinch of red (cayenne) pepper
3/4 cup whipping cream, whipped

To garnish:
2 tablespoons canned condensed consommé
2 tablespoons dairy sour cream
4 mushrooms, thinly sliced

Preparation and cooking time: 1 hour, including cooling

1. Preheat oven to 425F (220C). Divide pastry into 3 equal pieces. Roll each piece to a 10" x 5" rectangle. Rinse a baking sheet with cold water; place pastry rectangles on damp baking sheet. Prick pastry with a fork.
2. Bake pastry in preheated oven 12 to 15 minutes or until puffed and golden brown. Cool on a wire rack.
3. Prepare filling while pastry is cooking. Melt 3 tablespoons butter or margarine in a medium saucepan over medium heat. Stir in flour; cook 1 minute. Gradually stir in milk. Bring to a boil; simmer 3 minutes, stirring constantly. Remove from heat; place saucepan in a bowl of cold water. Let cool.
4. In a medium bowl, beat remaining butter or margarine until softened. Stir in shrimp, reserving 6 for garnish. Fold shrimp mixture into cooled sauce. If sauce is not completely cool, the butter or margarine will melt. Stir in lemon juice, hot-pepper sauce, salt, white pepper, red pepper and whipped cream.
5. Sandwich pastry layers together with shrimp filling.
6. In a small bowl, beat consommé and sour cream until smooth. Spread over top of filled pastry; arrange sliced mushrooms and reserved shrimp down center of sour-cream topping. Refrigerate until served. Do not assemble more than 1 hour before serving to prevent a soggy pastry. Makes 4 servings.

Shrimp Mille-Feuille

Chicken Goulash

6 to 8 chicken-breast halves, skinned
Salt
Freshly ground pepper
4 teaspoons paprika
2 tablespoons vegetable oil
2 medium onions, thinly sliced
2 green bell peppers, sliced
3 tablespoons tomato paste
1-1/4 cups plain yogurt
6 oz. mushrooms, sliced

To garnish:
Parsley sprigs

Preparation and cooking time: 1 hour

1. Sprinkle chicken with salt, pepper and 1 teaspoon paprika. Heat oil in a large skillet over medium heat. Add chicken; sauté 3 minutes per side.
2. Remove chicken with tongs; set aside. Add onions and bell peppers; sauté 4 minutes, stirring once or twice. Stir in remaining paprika, tomato paste and yogurt.
3. Return chicken to skillet; bring sauce to a boil. Reduce heat; cover. Simmer 35 minutes, turning chicken once.
4. Add mushrooms; cook 10 minutes or until chicken is tender. Garnish with parsley sprigs.
5. Serve with hot cooked rice or noodles tossed with butter or margarine and 1 teaspoon caraway seeds. Makes 4 servings.

Beef Strips in Red Wine

3 tablespoons butter or margarine
1 tablespoon vegetable oil
4 oz. mushrooms, sliced
1 medium onion, chopped
2 tablespoons all-purpose flour
Salt
Freshly ground pepper
1/2 teaspoon Italian seasoning
1-1/2 lb. beef round steak, cut into thin strips
1 garlic clove, crushed
1 tablespoon port
1/2 cup beef stock
1/2 cup red wine

Preparation and cooking time: 50 minutes

1. Heat butter or margarine and oil in a large skillet over medium heat. Add mushrooms; sauté 2 minutes. Remove cooked mushrooms with a slotted spoon; set aside. Add onion to skillet; sauté 4 minutes, stirring once or twice. Remove cooked onions with a slotted spoon; set aside.
2. In a plastic bag, combine flour, salt, pepper and Italian seasoning. Add beef, shake to coat. Shake excess flour from beef; add to fat remaining in skillet. Sauté 5 minutes, stirring frequently.
3. Stir in cooked mushrooms, cooked onions, garlic, port, stock and wine; bring to a boil.
4. Reduce heat to low. Cover pan; simmer 25 minutes.
5. Serve with boiled new potatoes and a green vegetable. Makes 4 servings.

Tandoori-Style Chicken

4 chicken legs with thighs attached, skinned
1 teaspoon salt
1 garlic clove, crushed
1 tablespoon tomato paste
1 tablespoon curry powder
2 bay leaves, finely crumbled
Juice of 1/2 lemon
1 (16-oz.) carton plain yogurt (2 cups)
6 tablespoons butter or margarine, melted
2 tablespoons paprika

To garnish:
1 lemon, quartered
Watercress sprigs

Preparation and cooking time: 1 hour

1. Preheat oven to 400F (205C). Slash chicken in several places with a sharp knife. Place chicken pieces in a casserole large enough to hold chicken in 1 layer.
2. In a small bowl, combine salt, garlic, tomato paste, curry powder, bay leaves and lemon juice; stir in yogurt. Pour yogurt mixture over chicken. Top with melted butter or margarine. Cover casserole.
3. Bake in preheated oven 50 minutes or until chicken is tender.
4. Pour off sauce; keep warm. Sprinkle paprika over baked chicken. Bake, uncovered, 5 minutes. Garnish with lemon and watercress. Serve sauce separately.
5. Serve with side dishes of bell-pepper rings, thin onion rings, banana slices dipped in lemon juice and rolled in shredded coconut and orange slices. Makes 4 servings.

Variation
To improve flavor, pour yogurt mixture over chicken; cover and refrigerate overnight. Add melted butter or margarine immediately before baking chicken.

Clockwise from top left: Tandoori-Style Chicken with coconut-coated banana slices, bell-pepper rings and onion rings; Beef Strips in Red Wine; Chicken Goulash

Beef Fricassee

1-1/2 lb. beef stew cubes, cut into 1-inch cubes
3 tablespoons butter or margarine
1 tablespoon vegetable oil
2 medium onions, thinly sliced
1 garlic clove, crushed
Grated peel of 1 lemon
1 tablespoon all-purpose flour
1 cup hot chicken stock
Salt
Freshly ground pepper
3 egg yolks
3 tablespoons lemon juice
1 tablespoon chopped fresh parsley

Preparation and cooking time: 1 hour

1. Trim off and discard any fat from beef.
2. In a large skillet, heat butter or margarine and oil over medium heat. Add onions and garlic; sauté 3 to 4 minutes. Remove with a slotted spoon.
3. Add beef to fat remaining in skillet; sauté until brown. Stir in lemon peel and flour; cook 1 minute.
4. Gradually stir in stock; season with salt and pepper. Return onions and garlic to skillet; bring to a boil. Reduce heat; cover. Simmer 45 minutes or until beef is tender.
5. In a small bowl, beat egg yolks and lemon juice; stir in 1/4 cup of stock mixture. Pour egg mixture into skillet. Stir well; heat about 4 minutes. Do not boil.
6. Garnish with parsley. Serve hot. Serve with broccoli, cauliflower or Brussels sprouts and new potatoes. Makes 4 servings.

Honeyed Lamb

1-1/2 lb. lamb stew cubes, cut into 1-inch cubes
2 medium onions, sliced
2 medium carrots, sliced
2 celery stalks, thinly sliced
1/2 teaspoon dried leaf thyme
1/2 cup cider or apple juice
2 tablespoons honey
1 tablespoon red-wine vinegar
Salt
Freshly ground pepper
1/2 tablespoon butter or margarine, room temperature
1 teaspoon all-purpose flour

Preparation and cooking time: 1 hour

1. Preheat oven to 400F (205C). Trim off and discard any fat from lamb. Place onions, carrots and celery into a 2-quart casserole; top with lamb cubes. Sprinkle with thyme.
2. In a small saucepan, heat cider or apple juice and honey. When honey dissolves, stir in vinegar; pour over lamb and vegetables. Season with salt and pepper. Cover casserole.
3. Bake in preheated oven 45 minutes or until lamb is tender.
4. In a small bowl, beat butter and flour to a smooth paste. Stir paste into cooking juices in casserole; bake 5 minutes.
5. Serve with mashed potatoes. Makes 4 servings.

Pork Chops in Normandy Sauce

4 pork chops
2 tablespoons butter or margarine
1 tablespoon vegetable oil
2 medium onions, sliced
1 garlic clove, crushed
2 medium cooking apples, peeled, thickly sliced
1/2 teaspoon dried leaf thyme
1 cup cider or apple juice
1 tablespoon honey
1 tablespoon brandy, if desired
Salt
Freshly ground pepper
1/4 cup whipping cream

Preparation and cooking time: 1 hour

1. Preheat oven to 375F (190C). Trim excess fat from chops. Heat 1 tablespoon butter or margarine and oil in a large skillet over medium heat. Add chops; sauté 3 minutes per side. Transfer to a shallow casserole large enough to hold chops in 1 layer.
2. Add remaining butter or margarine to skillet. Add onions and garlic; sauté over medium heat 3 minutes. Transfer to casserole with a slotted spoon.
3. Add apple slices; sauté 1 minute per side. Transfer to casserole with a slotted spoon.
4. Add thyme, cider or apple juice, honey and brandy, if desired to skillet. Season with salt and pepper. Stir until honey melts. Pour mixture over pork chops. Cover casserole.
5. Bake in preheated oven 35 minutes or until chops are tender. Skim fat from surface; stir in cream. Serve hot.
6. Serve with fresh vegetables, such as tiny carrots, whole green beans or green peas. Makes 4 servings.

Meatballs in Horseradish Sauce

1 bread slice
1/4 cup water
1 lb. lean ground beef
Salt
Freshly ground pepper
1/4 teaspoon dry mustard
1 egg, beaten
3 tablespoons butter or margarine

Sauce:
2 teaspoons all-purpose flour
1 cup chicken stock
2 tablespoons prepared horseradish sauce
1/2 teaspoon lemon juice

To garnish:
1 tablespoon chopped fresh parsley

Preparation and cooking time: 50 minutes

1. In a small bowl, soak bread in water a few minutes; squeeze dry.
2. In a medium bowl, combine soaked bread and ground beef, mashing it vigorously with a wooden spoon until it forms a paste. Beat in salt, pepper, dry mustard and egg. Or, place all ingredients in a food processor fitted with a steel blade; process until blended.
3. With floured hands, shape meat mixture into balls about 1-1/2 inches in diameter. Melt butter or margarine in a large skillet. Add meatballs; sauté 6 to 8 minutes or until brown and crisp, turning frequently. Remove meatballs from skillet with a slotted spoon; drain on paper towels.
4. To prepare sauce, stir flour into fat remaining in skillet; cook 1 minute. Gradually stir in stock. Bring to a boil; stir in horseradish sauce and lemon juice. Season with salt and pepper.
5. Return meatballs to pan. Cover and simmer over low heat 3 minutes.
6. Garnish with parsley; serve hot. Makes 4 servings.

Left to right: Beef Fricassee, Meatballs in Horseradish Sauce

Orange Bread & Butter Pudding

1/4 cup butter or margarine, room temperature
6 thin bread slices, crusts removed
Grated peel of 2 oranges
1/3 cup raisins
2 eggs, separated
2-1/2 cups milk
3 tablespoons sugar
1/4 teaspoon ground cinnamon
1/2 teaspoon vanilla extract

To decorate:
1 orange, thinly sliced
2 tablespoons red-currant jelly

To serve:
1 cup sweetened whipped cream

Preparation and cooking time: 1 hour

1. Preheat oven to 375F (190C). Grease a 1-quart baking dish.
2. Spread butter or margarine on bread; cut each slice into 4 triangles. Arrange triangles on bottom of greased baking dish. Sprinkle with grated orange peel and raisins.
3. In a medium bowl, beat egg yolks, milk, sugar, cinnamon and vanilla until blended. In a medium bowl, beat egg whites until stiff but not dry. Fold beaten egg whites into milk mixture; pour over bread.
4. Bake in preheated oven 40 to 45 minutes or until pudding has risen and is golden brown.
5. Arrange orange slices on top of pudding. Spoon jelly over orange slices. Serve pudding hot with sweetened whipped cream. Makes 4 servings.

Clockwise from left: Orange Bread & Butter Pudding, Steamed Lemon & Raisin Pudding, Crepe Gâteau with Cherry Sauce

Crepe Gâteau with Cherry Sauce

1-1/4 cups all-purpose flour
1/4 cup sugar
1/4 teaspoon salt
3 eggs
1-1/2 cups milk
1/3 cup unsalted butter or margarine, melted
Butter or margarine for cooking crepes

Cherry Sauce:
1 cup grape juice
1 cup water
2 tablespoons honey
1 tablespoon lemon juice
1 lb. fresh or frozen dark sweet cherries, pitted
1/4 cup cornstarch

To serve:
Sweetened whipped cream, if desired

Preparation and cooking time: 45 minutes, plus 1 hour standing

1. Place flour, sugar, salt, eggs and milk in a blender or food processor fitted with a steel blade; process until smooth, scraping down sides as necessary. With motor running, pour melted butter slowly into batter; process until combined. Pour batter into a large measuring cup or small pitcher. Cover and refrigerate 1 hour.
2. To prepare sauce, combine grape juice, water, honey and lemon juice in a medium saucepan. Add cherries; bring to a boil. Simmer 10 minutes or until cherries are softened.
3. Remove cherries with a slotted spoon; set aside. Pour liquid into a 2-cup measuring cup; add enough water to make 2 cups. In a small bowl, stir enough liquid into cornstarch to make a smooth paste. Pour liquid mixture into saucepan; stir in cornstarch mixture. Stir until blended. Cook over medium heat until sauce boils. Boil 2 minutes or until sauce clears and thickens, stirring constantly. Return cherries to sauce; set aside.
4. To cook crepes, melt 1 tablespoon butter or margarine in a 6- or 7-inch skillet or crepe pan. Pour in just enough batter to cover bottom of pan in a thin layer. Cook over medium heat 1-1/2 minutes or until small bubbles begin to form on surface of crepe. Turn crepe; cook 1-1/2 minutes. Remove to a flat plate; repeat process with remaining batter. Add additional butter or margarine to skillet as necessary.
5. Gently reheat sauce. Line up 4 serving plates. Place 1 crepe on each plate. Spoon a little sauce over each crepe. Repeat with 3 more crepes and more sauce on each plate, making a stack of 4 crepes with sauce between each layer.
6. Serve warm with remaining sauce on the side and sweetened whipped cream, if desired.

Variation
Substitute 1 (17-ounce) can pitted dark sweet cherries for fresh cherries. Use cherry juice instead of grape juice, adding as much water as necessary. Do not add cherries to sauce in step 2, but add them at the end of step 3. There will be fewer cherries in the sauce, but it will still be delicious.

Steamed Lemon & Raisin Puddings

3/4 cup all-purpose flour
1-1/2 teaspoons baking powder
1/2 cup sugar
1/2 cup butter or margarine, room temperature
2 eggs
Grated peel of 2 lemons
3 tablespoons lemon juice
2/3 cup raisins

Sauce:
1/4 cup honey
Grated peel of 2 lemons
1/4 cup lemon juice
2 tablespoons water
3 tablespoons raisins
1 tablespoon dark rum or brandy, if desired

To decorate:
Lemon slices

Preparation and cooking time: 1 hour

1. Grease 6 (5-ounce) dariole molds or ramekins. Sift flour and baking powder into a medium bowl. Add sugar, butter or margarine, eggs, lemon peel and lemon juice; beat until blended and smooth. Stir in raisins.
2. Spoon mixture into greased molds or ramekins. Cover tops with greased foil. Place molds on a trivet in a large saucepan. Add enough boiling water to come halfway up sides of molds. Bring to a boil. Cover; reduce heat until water simmers. Simmer 40 to 45 minutes, adding more water as necessary to maintain water level.
3. To prepare sauce, combine honey, lemon peel, lemon juice, water, raisins and rum or brandy, if desired, in a small saucepan. Cook over low heat 5 to 6 minutes, stirring constantly.
4. Run tip of a knife around inside edge of each mold; invert on a serving plate. Remove molds. Spoon a little sauce over puddings. Serve remaining sauce separately. Decorate with lemon slices. Makes 6 servings.

Braised Veal with Artichoke Hearts

6 tablespoons butter or margarine
1 lb. veal stew cubes, cut into 1-inch cubes
1 small onion, thinly sliced
1 garlic clove, crushed
2 oz. button mushrooms, sliced
1 teaspoon dried rosemary, crumbled
2/3 cup white wine or apple juice
1 (10-oz.) pkg. frozen artichoke hearts, thawed, halved
Salt
Freshly ground pepper
1 teaspoon all-purpose flour
1/4 cup whipping cream

Preparation and cooking time: 1 hour

1. Preheat oven to 325F (165C). Melt 3 tablespoons butter or margarine in a large skillet over medium heat. Add veal cubes; sauté 4 minutes or until browned. Transfer to a 2-quart flameproof casserole with a slotted spoon.
2. Add onion and garlic to fat remaining in skillet; sauté 2 minutes. Stir in mushrooms; sauté 2 minutes. Transfer to casserole with a slotted spoon.
3. Add rosemary, wine or apple juice and artichoke hearts to skillet; bring to a boil. Season with salt and pepper. Pour mixture into casserole.
4. Bake in preheated oven 30 minutes or until veal is tender.
5. In a small bowl, beat flour and remaining 3 tablespoons butter or margarine to a smooth paste. Stir paste into hot casserole; bring to a boil on top of stove. Simmer 2 to 3 minutes or until sauce has thickened.
6. Stir in cream; heat through. Do not boil. Serve with new potatoes and a green vegetable. Makes 4 servings.

To make ahead:
Prepare through step 4. Cool 30 minutes. Cover and refrigerate up to 2 days.

To serve:
Reheat casserole in preheated 325F (160C) oven 25 to 30 minutes. Complete steps 5 and 6 as directed.

Pork & Apricot Casserole

1-3/4 lb. lean pork
2 tablespoons all-purpose flour
Salt
Freshly ground pepper
1 teaspoon dried leaf thyme
1/4 cup olive oil
2 medium onions, sliced
1 garlic clove, crushed
4 celery stalks, thinly sliced
1 cup chicken stock
8 oz. dried apricots, soaked overnight
    in 1 cup orange juice

To garnish:
2 teaspoons chopped fresh parsley

Preparation and cooking time: 1 hour 15 minutes, plus overnight soaking

1. Preheat oven to 350F (175C). Trim pork; cut into 1" x 1/2" slices. In a plastic bag, combine flour, salt, pepper and thyme. Add pork slices; shake to coat in seasoned flour.
2. Heat oil in a large skillet over medium heat. Add coated pork slices; sauté about 8 minutes, turning to brown evenly. Transfer to a 2-quart casserole with a slotted spoon. Add onions, garlic and celery to fat remaining in skillet; sauté 4 minutes. Transfer vegetables to casserole with a slotted spoon.
3. Stir chicken stock into skillet; add apricots and orange juice; bring to a boil. Pour sauce over pork and vegetables; season with salt and pepper.
4. Bake in preheated oven 45 minutes or until pork and vegetables are tender.
5. Garnish with parsley. Serve with hot cooked rice and a green vegetable such as green beans or broccoli spears. Makes 4 servings.

To make ahead:
Prepare casserole through step 4. Cool 30 minutes. Cover and refrigerate up to 1 day.

To serve:
Reheat casserole in preheated 325F (165C) oven 30 minutes. Garnish with parsley.

Pork & Apricot Casserole

Stuffed Eggplant

4 medium eggplants
Salt
8 oz. bulk pork sausage
1 small onion, finely chopped
2 tablespoons raisins
2 large tomatoes, peeled, chopped
1/2 teaspoon ground coriander
2 tablespoons chopped fresh parsley
Freshly ground pepper
6 tablespoons olive oil
1/4 cup chicken stock or water

Preparation and cooking time: 1 hour 15 minutes, plus chilling

1. Cut eggplants in half lengthwise. Using a teaspoon or melon baller, scoop out pulp, leaving about 1/4-inch-thick walls. Put eggplant pulp in a colander; sprinkle with salt. Sprinkle eggplant shells with salt; place cut-side down in colander. Let drain 30 minutes.
2. Preheat oven to 350F (175C). To make filling, in a medium bowl, combine sausage, onion, raisins, tomatoes, coriander, 1 tablespoon parsley, salt and pepper.
3. Rinse salted eggplants; pat dry with paper towels. Chop eggplant pulp; stir into meat mixture. Spoon meat mixture into shells; pack firmly.
4. Arrange filled eggplant in 1 layer in a shallow baking dish; pour olive oil and stock or water around eggplant.
5. Bake, uncovered, in preheated oven 45 to 50 minutes or until eggplant is tender.
6. Serve hot. Or, let cool in baking dish. Cover and refrigerate. Garnish with remaining parsley.
7. Serve cold as a hearty first course. Or, serve hot as a main course with buttered potatoes and a green vegetable or salad. Makes 4 servings.

To make ahead:
Prepare through step 5. Cover and refrigerate up to 24 hours.

To serve:
To serve cold, transfer to a serving dish; garnish with parsley. To serve hot, reheat in preheated 325F (160C) oven 30 minutes or until heated through.

Potted Ham

10 oz. lean cooked ham
1/2 cup unsalted butter, melted, cooled
1/4 cup whipping cream
1 tablespoon chopped fresh parsley
1 teaspoon prepared brown mustard
2 tablespoons dry sherry
Pinch of ground nutmeg
Freshly ground pepper

To garnish:
1 red bell pepper

To serve:
8 bread slices

Preparation time: 20 minutes, plus chilling

1. Trim excess fat from ham. Grind ham in a meat grinder or process in a food processor fitted with a steel blade until coarsely chopped.
2. In a medium bowl, stir 1/2 of butter into ham. Stir in cream, parsley, mustard and sherry. Season with nutmeg and pepper.
3. Spoon mixture into a 2-cup straight-sided serving dish or terrine; pack down firmly with the back of a spoon.
4. Pour remaining butter over ham mixture, remelting butter if necessary. Tip dish to spread butter over top of mixture.
5. Cover dish with foil or plastic wrap; refrigerate until chilled.
6. Quarter red pepper; discard seeds and stem. Cut pepper into small diamond or leaf shapes. Garnish top of dish with pepper shapes.
7. Toast bread; cut into triangles. Serve hot with potted ham.
8. Serve potted ham as a first course or as a light lunch or supper dish with salad. Makes 4 main-dish servings.

To make ahead:
Prepare potted ham as above. Cover and refrigerate up to 2 days. Cut pepper shapes for garnish immediately before serving.

To serve:
Arrange garnish on dish. Make toast.

Blue-Cheese Mousse

2 cups crumbled blue cheese or Roquefort cheese (8 oz.)
1 (1/4-oz.) envelope plus 1 teaspoon unflavored gelatin
1/4 cup cold water
2 eggs, separated
1 tablespoon Worcestershire sauce
1/2 cup finely chopped walnuts
1/2 pint whipping cream (1 cup)

To garnish:
1 small cucumber, thinly sliced
8 walnut halves
Watercress sprigs

Preparation time: 30 minutes, plus chilling

1. Brush inside of a 4- to 5-cup mold with vegetable oil. In a blender or food processor fitted with a steel blade, process cheese until almost smooth. Spoon into a medium bowl.
2. In a small saucepan, combine gelatin and cold water. Stir well; let stand 3 minutes. Stir over low heat until gelatin dissolves; set aside to cool.
3. In a medium bowl, beat egg yolks until creamy. Stir in Worcestershire sauce and walnuts. Stir into cheese. Stir in cooled gelatin mixture.
4. In a medium bowl, whip cream until stiff peaks form. Stir 3 to 4 tablespoons into cheese mixture to lighten. Fold in remaining whipped cream.
5. In another medium bowl, beat egg whites until stiff but not dry. Fold beaten egg whites into cheese mixture.
6. Spoon mixture into oiled mold. Refrigerate several hours or until set.
7. With tip of a sharp knife, loosen mousse from mold. Invert mold on a serving plate. Rinse a dish towel in hot water; wring dry. Wrap hot towel around outside of mold; let stand 30 seconds. Remove mold. Arrange cucumber slices around mousse. Decorate top with walnut halves; garnish with watercress sprigs. Makes 4 servings.

To make ahead:
Prepare mousse through step 6. Cover and refrigerate up to 24 hours.

To serve:
Turn out mousse; garnish as directed in step 7.

Left to right: Stuffed Eggplant, Potted Ham, Blue-Cheese Mousse

Haddock Casserole with Garlic Sauce

1-1/2 lb. fresh haddock fillets
3 tablespoons olive oil
2 large onions, sliced
2 garlic cloves, crushed
1 (15-oz.) can tomatoes
1 tablespoon chopped fresh parsley
1 tablespoon chopped fresh mint or 1 teaspoon dried
  leaf mint
1/2 cup water
1 cup dry white wine
2 bay leaves
2 parsley sprigs
1 (4-inch) orange-peel strip
3 cups diced, peeled potatoes (1 lb.)
Salt
Freshly ground pepper

Garlic Sauce:
1/4 cup mayonnaise
2 garlic cloves, crushed
1 tablespoon tomato paste
1 tablespoon chopped fresh mint or 1 teaspoon dried
  leaf mint

Preparation and cooking time: 1 hour 15 minutes

1. Trim fish; cut into 3-inch pieces.
2. Heat olive oil in a 2-quart flameproof casserole. Add onions and garlic; sauté over low heat 8 to 10 minutes, stirring occasionally. Add tomatoes with juice, parsley and mint; increase heat to medium. Cook 10 minutes.
3. Add water, wine, bay leaves, parsley and orange peel. Bring to a boil.
4. Add potatoes, salt and pepper. Cover casserole; simmer 20 minutes. Add fish; simmer 8 to 10 minutes or until fish tests done. Do not overcook. Discard bay leaves, parsley and orange peel.
5. To prepare sauce, in a small bowl, combine ingredients until blended. Serve sauce separately. Makes 4 servings.

To make ahead:
This dish improves in flavor during refrigeration. Slightly undercook. Cool 30 minutes. Cover and refrigerate up to 24 hours. Cover and refrigerate sauce up to 2 days.

To serve:
Reheat casserole over low heat about 15 minutes. Bring almost to a boil.

Left to right: Haddock Casserole with Garlic Sauce, Pickled Herring

Pickled Herring

8 herring fillets
1/2 cup water
1/2 cup red-wine vinegar
6 to 8 peppercorns
2 bay leaves

To garnish:
1 small onion, sliced into rings
2 small pickles, thinly sliced
1 red bell pepper, thinly sliced
1 orange, thinly sliced

Preparation and cooking time: 1 hour, plus cooling

1. Preheat oven to 350F (175C). Rinse fillets; pat dry with paper towels. Roll up fillets, skin-side out. Secure with wooden picks.
2. Arrange fillets in 1 layer in a shallow baking dish; add water, vinegar, peppercorns and bay leaves. Cover dish with foil.
3. Bake in preheated oven 10 to 12 minutes or until fish tests done.
4. Let fish cool in cooking liquid. Cover and refrigerate up to 3 days.
5. To serve, transfer to a serving dish, discarding liquid, peppercorns and bay leaves. Garnish with onion, pickles, bell pepper and orange.
6. Serve with crusty whole-wheat bread. Makes 4 servings.

To make ahead:
This dish must be prepared in advance so that herring has time to cool. Prepare through step 4. Cover and refrigerate up to 3 days.

To serve:
Garnish as directed in step 5.

Make-Ahead Chili

8 oz. bulk Italian pork sausage
8 oz. lean ground beef
2 garlic cloves, minced
1 large onion, chopped
1 (16-oz.) can chopped tomatoes
1 (16-oz.) can red-kidney beans
1 tablespoon chili powder
1/2 teaspoon cumin
1/2 teaspoon red (cayenne) pepper, if desired

To serve:
Cooked spaghetti or rice
Chopped onion
Shredded sharp Cheddar cheese

Preparation and cooking time: 1 hour

1. Preheat oven to 350F (175C).
2. Cook Italian sausage and ground beef in a large skillet over medium heat, stirring, until browned. With a slotted spoon, transfer cooked meat to a 1-1/2-quart casserole; set aside.
3. Remove and discard all fat except about 2 tablespoons. Add garlic and onion; sauté about 4 minutes. Add to meat with tomatoes and undrained kidney beans. Stir well. Stir in chili powder, cumin and red pepper.
4. Bake in preheated oven 25 minutes or until hot and bubbly.
5. Serve over spaghetti or rice; top with chopped onion and Cheddar cheese. Makes 4 servings.

To make ahead:
Make chili through step 4. Cool 30 minutes. Cover and refrigerate up to 2 days.

To serve:
Reheat, uncovered, in preheated 350F (175C) oven until hot and bubbly.

Coriander Lamb with Orange Rice

1/4 cup butter or margarine
3 large onions, finely chopped
2 bay leaves, finely crumbled
6 tablespoons water
1-1/2 lb. lamb stew cubes, cut into 1-inch cubes
2 garlic cloves, crushed
1 (1/2-inch) piece fresh gingerroot, peeled, finely chopped
1 tablespoon ground coriander
1 teaspoon ground cumin
2 teaspoons paprika
About 1/2 teaspoon red (cayenne) pepper
1 teaspoon salt
1/2 cup plain yogurt
1-1/2 cups diced, peeled potatoes (8 oz.)
2 teaspoons lemon juice
4 large tomatoes, peeled, quartered

To serve:
1 lemon, quartered

Orange Rice:
1 tablespoon vegetable oil
1-1/3 cups uncooked long-grain white rice
1 teaspoon ground turmeric
2-2/3 cups chicken stock or water
1 teaspoon salt
1 orange
2 tablespoons blanched almonds, toasted
1 tablespoon chopped fresh parsley

Preparation and cooking time: 2 hours 15 minutes

1. Preheat oven to 350F (175C). Melt 2 tablespoons butter or margarine in a large skillet over medium heat. Add onions and bay leaves; sauté 8 to 10 minutes or until lightly browned, stirring frequently. Stir in 1 tablespoon water. Transfer mixture to a 2-1/2-quart casserole.
2. Melt remaining butter or margarine in skillet. Add lamb; sauté about 5 minutes or until browned. Transfer browned lamb to casserole.
3. Add garlic and ginger to fat remaining in skillet; sauté 2 minutes. Stir in spices; cook 1 minute. Stir in remaining water, salt and yogurt; slowly bring to a boil. Add to casserole. Cover casserole.
4. Bake in preheated oven 30 minutes. Add potatoes and lemon juice; bake 45 minutes or until lamb and potatoes are tender.
5. Add tomatoes; bake 5 minutes. Serve with lemon wedges.
6. About 30 minutes before lamb dish is ready, prepare Orange Rice. To prepare rice, heat oil in a medium sauce-pan over medium heat. Stir in rice; cook 1 minute. Stir in turmeric; gradually stir in stock or water and salt. Cover pan; simmer 20 minutes or until rice is tender.
7. While rice is cooking, grate orange peel. Peel orange; cut into sections with a small sharp knife.
8. Let rice stand 5 minutes before serving. Stir in orange peel, orange sections and almonds. Garnish with parsley. Makes 4 servings.

To make ahead:
Prepare casserole through step 4. Cool 30 minutes; cover and refrigerate up to 2 days. Toast almonds.

To serve:
Reheat casserole in preheated 325F (160C) oven 30 minutes. Complete steps 5 through 8 as directed above.

Left to right: Coriander Lamb with Orange Rice, Pork in Curry Sauce

Pork in Curry Sauce

2 pork-loin tenderloins, about 1-1/2 lb. total weight
1 cup plain yogurt
2 teaspoons curry powder
1 teaspoon ground turmeric
1 teaspoon salt
1/2 teaspoon freshly ground pepper
1/2 teaspoon paprika
1/4 cup butter or margarine
1 medium onion, finely chopped
2 garlic cloves, crushed
3 tablespoons ground almonds
2 cups shredded coconut
1 cup boiling water

To garnish:
1 large lemon, thinly sliced
2 large, firm tomatoes, thinly sliced

To serve:
Hot cooked rice
Mango or peach chutney
Pita-bread rounds
Shredded coconut
Sliced bananas
Raisins

Preparation and cooking time: 2 hours 25 minutes, plus marinating

1. Trim tenderloins, cutting off thin ends; reserve for other use. Place trimmed tenderloins in a shallow pan large enough to hold them in 1 layer.
2. In a small bowl, combine yogurt, curry powder, turmeric, salt, pepper and paprika. Pour mixture over pork; turn to coat thoroughly with marinade. Cover and refrigerate 1 hour.
3. Melt butter or margarine in a large saucepan over medium heat. Add onion and garlic; sauté 4 minutes, stirring once or twice.
4. Add pork and yogurt marinade. Bring to a simmer; simmer 5 minutes. Stir in ground almonds. Cook over very low heat 1-1/2 hours, turning meat in sauce occasionally. If your stove does not maintain a very low heat, use a heat diffuser on the heating unit.
5. Place coconut in a small bowl; add boiling water. Let stand 10 minutes. Line a sieve with cheesecloth; place over a medium bowl. Pour coconut and liquid into sieve. Press with a wooden spoon to extract all liquid.
6. Stir coconut liquid into sauce in pan; simmer 10 minutes.
7. To serve, cut deep slits crosswise in cooked tenderloins about 1-1/4 inches apart. Cut lemon slices in halves. Arrange lemon slices and tomato slices alternately in slits.
8. The sauce in this dish is thin. If a thicker sauce is desired, simmer until reduced or stir in a little cornstarch and water mixture.
9. To serve, accompany with hot cooked rice, chutney, pita bread, coconut, bananas and raisins. Makes 4 servings.

To make ahead:
Prepare dish to end of step 6. Cool 30 minutes. Cover and refrigerate up to 2 days.

To serve:
Reheat over low heat. Complete steps 7 through 9.

Ham & Cheese Crepes

8 crepes, recipe opposite
8 cooked-ham slices
8 slices Monterey Jack cheese or Swiss cheese
1 (15-oz.) can asparagus spears, drained
1 chopped canned pimento
1 (10-3/4-oz.) can condensed cream of mushroom soup
1/2 cup half and half
1 (4-oz.) can sliced mushrooms, drained
1/2 teaspoon dried marjoram
Freshly ground pepper

Preparation and cooking time: 35 minutes

1. Preheat oven to 400F (205C). Grease a 13" x 9" pan.
2. Place a ham slice on each crepe. Top with a cheese slice, asparagus and pimento. Roll up crepes; place crepes, seam-side down, in greased pan.
3. Bake in preheated oven 20 minutes or until heated through.
4. While crepes are baking, make sauce. In a medium saucepan, combine mushroom soup, half and half, mushrooms, marjoram and pepper. Bring to a boil, stirring constantly. Pour sauce into a serving dish. Serve separately with hot crepes. Makes 4 servings.

To make ahead:
Make crepes using recipe opposite.

To serve:
Use prepared crepes. Prepare as directed above.

Quick Macaroni Casserole

1 (10-3/4-oz.) can condensed cream of mushroom soup
1 cup milk
2 cups diced cooked ham or tongue
2 cups cooked macaroni
2 hard-cooked eggs, chopped
4 oz. Cheddar cheese, diced
1 onion, chopped
1/2 cup chopped green bell pepper
1/2 cup chopped celery
1 (2-oz.) jar chopped pimento, well-drained
Salt
Freshly ground black pepper

To garnish:
Chopped parsley

Preparation and cooking time: 45 minutes

1. Preheat oven to 350F (175C).
2. Place mushroom soup in a large bowl; stir in milk until blended.
3. Stir in ham or tongue, macaroni, eggs, cheese, onion, bell pepper, celery, pimento, salt and black pepper. Spoon into a 1-1/2-quart casserole; cover with a lid or foil.
4. Bake in preheated oven 25 to 30 minutes or until hot and bubbly. Garnish with parsley. Makes 4 servings.

To make ahead:
Prepare casserole as directed above. Cool 30 minutes. Cover and refrigerate up to 2 days.

To serve:
Reheat in preheated 350F (175C) oven about 30 minutes or until hot and bubbly. Garnish with parsley.

Crepes

2 cups all-purpose flour
1/4 teaspoon salt
4 eggs
About 2 cups milk
1/4 cup butter or margarine, melted
Butter or margarine for cooking crepes

Preparation and cooking time: 1 hour 30 minutes, plus 1 hour for crepe batter to rest

1. In a large bowl, combine flour and salt. In a medium bowl, beat eggs with a whisk; beat in 2 cups milk until combined. Slowly pour egg mixture into flour, beating constantly. Beat until mixture is blended and batter is smooth. Slowly add melted butter or margarine, beating until combined.
2. Or, place ingredients in a blender or food processor. Process 1 to 2 minutes or until batter is smooth.
3. Pour batter into a pitcher. Cover and refrigerate at least 1 hour.
4. Stir refrigerated batter. If batter has thickened slightly, stir in a few teaspoons milk.
5. Melt 1 teaspoon butter or margarine in a 6- or 7-inch skillet or crepe pan over medium heat. Pour in 3 tablespoons batter or enough to make a thin layer in bottom of pan. Cook over medium heat 1-1/2 minutes or until small bubbles begin to form on crepe's surface. With a spatula, turn crepe over; cook 1-1/2 minutes. Remove cooked crepe to a flat plate; repeat with remaining batter. Add more butter or margarine to skillet or pan as necessary.
6. Cool crepes. Refrigerate up to 2 days or freeze. Makes about 34 crepes.

To make ahead:
Prepare and cook crepes as directed above. Cool; place foil squares between each crepe. Refrigerate up to 2 days or freeze up to 2 months.

To serve:
Remove only as many crepes as needed. Crepes can be removed without thawing.

Southern Fried Chicken

2 (2- to 2-1/2-lb.) chickens, cut up
3/4 cup all-purpose flour
1-1/2 teaspoons salt
1 teaspoon poultry seasoning
2 teaspoons paprika
1 egg
1 tablespoon vegetable oil
1/4 cup shortening

Preparation and cooking time: 55 minutes, including standing time

1. Rinse chicken pieces; pat dry with paper towels.
2. Combine flour, salt, poultry seasoning and paprika in a plastic bag. Beat egg with 1 tablespoon oil in a small bowl.
3. Dip chicken, 1 piece at a time, in egg mixture. Shake off excess liquid; place in flour mixture. Shake to coat chicken piece completely. Repeat with remaining chicken. Place coated chicken pieces on waxed paper; let stand about 20 minutes.
4. Heat shortening in a large skillet over medium heat. Add chicken pieces; cook until browned on all sides, turning chicken frequently with tongs. Do not crowd skillet; cook in batches, if necessary. Lower heat; cook about 20 minutes or until chicken is fork-tender. Dark meat will take longer to cook than white meat. Drain on paper towels.
5. Serve immediately or cover and refrigerate until ready to serve. Makes 4 to 6 servings.

To make ahead:
Prepare through step 4. Cool slightly. Cover loosely and refrigerate up to 2 days.

To serve:
Serve cold or reheat in preheated 350F (175C) oven 20 minutes or until hot.

Turkey Tetrazzini

2 tablespoons butter or margarine
8 oz. mushrooms, sliced
3 tablespoons all-purpose flour
1-1/4 cups chicken broth
1/2 cup half and half
1/4 cup dry sherry
Salt
Freshly ground pepper
2 cups diced cooked turkey or chicken
1 (8-oz.) pkg. thin spaghetti, cooked, drained
1/4 cup grated Parmesan cheese
Additional grated Parmesan cheese

Preparation and cooking time: 40 minutes

1. Preheat oven to 350F (175C). Grease a 2-1/2-quart casserole.
2. Heat butter or margarine in a medium saucepan. Add mushrooms; sauté 5 minutes over medium heat.
3. Sprinkle flour over mushrooms; stir well. Gradually stir in chicken broth. Stir in half and half; cook, stirring, until sauce thickens slightly. Remove from heat; stir in sherry, salt and pepper.
4. Place turkey or chicken and spaghetti in greased casserole; toss until combined. Pour sauce over spaghetti mixture; toss until combined. Sprinkle with 1/4 cup Parmesan cheese.
5. Bake in preheated oven 20 minutes or until hot and bubbly.
6. Serve with additional Parmesan cheese. Makes 4 servings.

To make ahead:
Prepare casserole through step 4. Cover and refrigerate up to 1 day.

To serve:
Bake in preheated 350F (175C) oven 30 minutes or until hot and bubbly.

Individual Chicken Packages

2 tablespoons vegetable oil
2 tablespoons butter or margarine
8 chicken legs
4 to 6 tablespoons honey
2 teaspoons ground ginger
Paprika
Salt
Freshly ground pepper

Preparation and cooking time: 1 hour 20 minutes

1. Preheat oven to 350F (175C).
2. Heat oil and butter or margarine in a large skillet. Add chicken legs; cook over medium heat until browned on all sides.
3. Cut 4 foil pieces, each large enough to wrap around 2 chicken legs. Place 2 browned chicken legs in center of each piece of foil.
4. Spoon honey over chicken; sprinkle with ginger, paprika, salt and pepper. Bring up sides of foil; press edges together to seal packages. Place on a baking sheet.
5. Bake in preheated oven 1 hour or until chicken is fork-tender.
6. Serve in packages. Makes 4 servings.

Variation
Substitute 4 chicken-breast halves for chicken legs. Reduce cooking time to 45 minutes.

To make ahead:
Prepare through step 5. Refrigerate packages, unopened, up to 2 days.

To serve:
Reheat in preheated 350F (175C) oven 20 to 30 minutes or until hot.

Zucchini Moussaka

1/4 cup olive oil
1-1/2 lb. zucchini, thinly sliced
1 large onion, thinly sliced
2 green bell peppers, sliced
1 garlic clove, crushed
1 lb. fresh tomatoes, peeled, sliced
1 tablespoon tomato paste
1 tablespoon chopped fresh mint
Salt
Freshly ground pepper
4 oz. Swiss cheese, thinly sliced
2 tablespoons all-purpose flour
1-1/4 cups plain yogurt
2 egg yolks
3/4 cup shredded Cheddar cheese (3 oz.)

Preparation and cooking time: 1 hour 15 minutes

1. Preheat oven to 400F (205C). Grease a shallow 2-quart casserole.
2. Heat oil in a medium skillet over medium heat. Add zucchini slices, a few at a time. Sauté until lightly browned. Remove sautéed zucchini with a slotted spoon; drain on paper towels. Repeat with remaining zucchini.
3. Add onion, bell peppers and garlic to skillet; sauté 4 minutes, stirring once or twice. Add a little more oil, if necessary. Stir in tomatoes, tomato paste, mint, salt and pepper. Cook 2 minutes.
4. Arrange 1/2 of zucchini in greased casserole. Cover with 1/2 of tomato mixture, then with Swiss cheese. Cover cheese with remaining tomato mixture; arrange remaining zucchini over tomato mixture.
5. In a medium bowl, combine flour, yogurt, egg yolks, Cheddar cheese, salt and pepper. Pour over zucchini. Place dish on a baking sheet.
6. Bake, uncovered, in preheated oven 25 minutes or until top is brown. Serve hot.
7. Serve with hot cooked rice or pasta. Makes 4 servings.

To make ahead:
Prepare casserole through step 4. Cover and refrigerate up to 1 day. Or, prepare through step 6. Cool and refrigerate.

To serve:
Complete steps 5 and 6. Or if baked ahead, reheat in preheated 375F (190C) oven 20 minutes.

Pork Chops in Red-Wine Sauce

4 large pork loin chops
1 garlic clove, finely chopped
2 tablespoons butter or margarine
2 small zucchini, sliced
6 oz. mushrooms, sliced
4 large tomatoes, peeled, sliced
1 tablespoon honey
1/2 cup red wine
1 tablespoon chopped fresh thyme or 1 teaspoon
   dried leaf thyme
Salt
Freshly ground pepper

To garnish:
1 tablespoon chopped fresh parsley

Preparation and cooking time: 1 hour

1. Preheat oven to 375F (190C). Trim excess fat from chops. Sauté chops and garlic in a nonstick skillet over medium heat 3 minutes per side. Transfer chops to a shallow casserole large enough to hold chops in 1 layer.
2. Melt butter or margarine in skillet; add zucchini and mushrooms. Sauté 2 minutes, stirring occasionally. Add sautéed vegetables to casserole.
3. Add tomatoes, honey, wine, thyme, salt and pepper to casserole.
4. Cover and bake in preheated oven 30 minutes.
5. Garnish with parsley. Serve with a salad of sliced green peppers, diced cucumber and sliced cabbage with French dressing and whole-wheat pasta tossed in melted butter or margarine and parsley. Makes 4 servings.

To make ahead:
Prepare casserole through step 4; cool 30 minutes. Cover and refrigerate up to 2 days.

To serve:
Reheat casserole in preheated 350F (175C) oven 30 minutes or until heated through. Garnish with parsley.

Clockwise from left: Buttered whole-wheat pasta, Pork Chops in Red-Wine Sauce, Zucchini Moussaka

Left to right: Honeycomb Mold, Gingersnap-Cream Roll,
Rose-Water Sponge Drops

Honeycomb Mold

1 (1/4-oz.) envelope unflavored gelatin (1 tablespoon)
1 pint whipping cream (2 cups)
2 eggs, separated
1/4 cup honey
1/2 teaspoon vanilla extract
1 pint raspberries

To decorate:
Mint leaves

Preparation time: 20 minutes, plus chilling

1. Combine gelatin and cream in top of a double boiler; stir over simmering water until gelatin is dissolved and little bubbles begin to form around edge.

2. In a small bowl, beat egg yolks and honey. Stir a little hot cream mixture into egg-yolk mixture, beating constantly. Return mixture to top of double boiler. Cook, stirring, about 4 minutes or until mixture coats back of a spoon. Remove from heat; stir in vanilla. Refrigerate until mixture mounds when dropped from a spoon.

3. Brush inside of a 4-cup decorative mold with vegetable oil; set aside. In a medium bowl, beat egg whites until stiff but not dry. Fold beaten egg whites into chilled honey mixture.

4. Pour honey mixture into oiled mold; smooth top. Refrigerate several hours or until set.

5. With tip of a sharp knife, carefully loosen dessert from edge of mold. Invert mold on a serving plate. Rinse a dish towel in hot water; wring dry. Wrap hot towel around outside of mold; let stand 30 seconds. Remove mold. Arrange raspberries around dessert; decorate with mint leaves. Makes 4 servings.

To make ahead:
Prepare dessert through step 4. Cover and refrigerate up to 2 days.

To serve:
Unmold and garnish as directed in step 5.

Gingersnap-Cream Roll

1 pint whipping cream (2 cups)
1/4 cup chopped mixed candied fruit
2 tablespoons sweet sherry, if desired
12 to 15 large gingersnaps

To decorate:
Fresh strawberries

Preparation time: 15 minutes, plus chilling

1. In a medium bowl, whip cream until stiff peaks form; stir in candied fruit and sherry, if desired.
2. Spread 1 side of cookies with 1/2 of cream mixture; arrange cookies into a long roll on a serving plate. Cover with remaining cream mixture.
3. Refrigerate several hours or overnight to allow cookies to soften and flavors to blend.
4. Slice strawberries; place in an overlapping row down center of cake. Makes 4 servings.

To make ahead:
Prepare roll through step 4. Cover and refrigerate up to 2 days.

To serve:
Decorate with strawberries as directed in step 4.

Almond-Mint Pie

Crust:
1 cup chocolate-cookie crumbs
1/2 cup ground almonds
1/4 cup sugar
1/4 cup butter or margarine, melted

Filling:
1 qt. mint chocolate-chip ice cream (4 cups)
2 tablespoons crème de menthe

To decorate:
2 cups sweetened whipped cream
Slivered almonds

Preparation time: 25 minutes, plus chilling

1. In a medium bowl, combine cookie crumbs, almonds and sugar. Pour in melted butter or margarine; stir until combined. Press crumb mixture onto side and bottom of a 9-inch pie pan. Refrigerate about 30 minutes or until chilled.
2. Spoon ice cream into a medium bowl; let stand at room temperature 10 minutes. Stir ice cream; spoon into chilled pie crust. Smooth top; sprinkle with crème de menthe. Place in freezer until ready to serve.
3. When ready to serve, cover top of pie with sweetened whipped cream; decorate with slivered almonds. Makes 6 servings.

To make ahead:
Prepare pie through step 2. Open freeze without wrapping. When frozen, wrap tightly in foil. Freeze up to 1 month.

To serve:
Let stand at room temperature 15 minutes. Decorate as directed in step 3.

Rose-Water Sponge Drops

2 eggs
1/2 cup sugar
2/3 cup all-purpose flour
1 teaspoon baking powder
1 tablespoon rose water

Filling:
Few drops rose water
1-1/2 cups sweetened whipped cream
Powdered sugar

Preparation and cooking time: 45 minutes, plus cooling

1. Preheat oven to 375F (190C). Grease baking sheets.
2. In a medium bowl, beat eggs and sugar until thick and creamy.
3. Sift flour and baking powder over egg mixture; gradually fold in. Stir in rose water.
4. Drop mixture by teaspoonfuls onto greased baking sheets, spacing about 1-1/2 inches apart.
5. Bake 6 to 8 minutes or until golden. Remove from baking sheets; cool completely on wire racks.
6. To prepare filling, stir rose water into sweetened whipped cream. Pipe whipped cream onto bottoms of 1/2 of sponge drops. Top with remaining sponge drops; dust with powdered sugar. Serve immediately to prevent drops from getting soggy. Makes 24 sponge drops.

To make ahead:
Prepare cookies through step 5. Store in an airtight container until ready to use or freeze up to 2 months.

To serve:
Finish cookies as directed in step 6.

Smoked-Mackerel & Cream-Cheese Pâté
Pork Chops with Marjoram Sauce
Small Potatoes tossed in Herb Butter
Green Peas
Raspberries in Melba Sauce

Pork Chops with Marjoram Sauce

2 tablespoons butter or margarine
1 tablespoon vegetable oil
4 large pork chops
1 medium onion, finely chopped
1 garlic clove, finely chopped
3 tablespoons chicken stock
3 tablespoons dry vermouth
1 tablespoon chopped fresh marjoram or 1 teaspoon
    dried leaf marjoram
Salt
Freshly ground pepper
1/4 cup whipping cream

Preparation and cooking time: 1 hour

1. Heat butter or margarine and oil in a flameproof casserole over medium heat. Add pork chops; sauté 4 minutes per side. Remove chops with tongs; keep warm.
2. Add onion and garlic to fat remaining in casserole. Sauté 3 minutes, stirring occasionally; stir in stock and vermouth. Return chops to casserole; add marjoram, salt and pepper.
3. Bring to a boil. Cover; reduce heat. Simmer 30 minutes or until pork chops are tender and no longer pink.
4. Increase heat; bring to a boil again. Boil until liquid is slightly reduced. Stir in cream; heat through. Makes 4 servings.

Raspberries in Melba Sauce

1 lb. raspberries, fresh or thawed frozen
Sauce:
12 oz. raspberries, fresh or thawed frozen
1 teaspoon lemon juice
1 cup powdered sugar, sifted

To serve:
1/4 teaspoon ground cinnamon
1/4 cup powdered sugar, sifted
2/3 cup whipping cream, whipped
1 egg white, stiffly beaten

Preparation time: 20 minutes, plus thawing time for frozen raspberries

1. Place 1 pound raspberries in a serving dish.
2. To prepare sauce, press 12 ounces raspberries through a sieve into a medium bowl. Stir lemon juice and 1 cup powdered sugar into puree. Pour over whole raspberries; gently stir to combine. Cover bowl and refrigerate until served.
3. To serve, stir cinnamon and 1/4 cup powdered sugar into whipped cream; fold in beaten egg white. Serve separately with raspberries. Make topping immediately before serving. Makes 4 servings.

Smoked-Mackerel & Cream-Cheese Pâté

1/2 cup butter or margarine, room temperature
2 (3-oz.) pkgs. cream cheese, room temperature
12 oz. smoked mackerel or other
    smoked fish, skinned, flaked
2 teaspoons lemon juice
1 tablespoon chopped chives
Freshly ground pepper

To garnish:
4 small bay leaves

Preparation time: 20 minutes

1. In a medium bowl, cream 6 tablespoons butter or margarine and cream cheese. Stir in fish, lemon juice, chives and pepper. Beat until mixture is smooth.
2. Divide pâté among 4 individual ramekin dishes; smooth tops. Melt remaining butter or margarine in a small saucepan. Pour melted butter or margarine over pâté. Tip dishes to form a thin, even layer. Garnish each pâté with a bay leaf.
3. Cover with plastic wrap; refrigerate up to 2 days. Makes 4 servings.

Clockwise from left: Pork Chop with Marjoram Sauce, Raspberries in Melba Sauce, Smoked-Mackerel & Cream-Cheese Pâté

Beef Paprika with Rice

2 tablespoons vegetable oil
1 medium onion, thinly sliced
1 garlic clove, crushed
2 celery stalks, thinly sliced
1 lb. lean ground beef
1 tablespoon all-purpose flour
1 tablespoon paprika
Salt
Freshly ground pepper
1 bay leaf
1 cup chicken stock
1-1/3 cups uncooked long-grain white rice
2 tablespoons butter or margarine
4 oz. button mushrooms, sliced
3 tablespoons dairy sour cream

To garnish:
1 tablespoon chopped fresh parsley

Preparation and cooking time: 1 hour 20 minutes

1. Heat oil in a large skillet over medium heat. Add onion, garlic and celery; sauté 4 minutes, stirring once or twice. Add ground beef; sauté 8 minutes, stirring to break up meat and brown evenly. Drain off excess fat. Stir in flour and paprika; cook 2 minutes.
2. Add salt, pepper, bay leaf and stock; bring to a boil. Cover; lower heat. Simmer about 50 minutes. Dish can be made ahead to this point and refrigerated, if desired.
3. Cook rice according to package directions while meat is simmering.
4. Melt butter or margarine in a small skillet over medium heat. Add mushrooms; sauté 3 to 4 minutes.
5. Remove bay leaf from meat. Stir in sour cream; heat through. Do not boil.
6. Spoon meat and sauce in the center of a heated serving dish; surround with hot cooked rice. Place mushrooms over meat; garnish with parsley. Serve with steamed spinach. Makes 4 servings.

Green Beans Greek-Style

1/4 cup olive oil
1 garlic clove, finely chopped
1 medium onion, finely chopped
1/2 cup dry white wine
1/2 cup water
1 tablespoon tomato paste
8 coriander seeds, crushed
Fresh parsley
Salt
Freshly ground pepper
1 lb. green beans, trimmed
4 oz. button mushrooms, sliced

Preparation and cooking time: 1 hour

1. Heat olive oil in a large saucepan over low heat. Add garlic and onion; sauté 10 minutes, stirring frequently. Add wine, water, tomato paste, coriander, parsley, salt and pepper. Bring to a boil. Cover; simmer 5 minutes.
2. Add beans and mushrooms. Cover; simmer 20 to 25 minutes or until beans are crisp-tender.
3. Spoon mixture into a serving dish; cool. Cover and refrigerate until served.
4. Serve chilled. Makes 4 servings.

Oranges in Raisin Syrup

1/4 cup honey
5 tablespoons water
1 tablespoon lemon juice
1/3 cup raisins
1 tablespoon dark rum, if desired
6 seedless oranges, peeled, thinly sliced

To decorate:
6 to 8 walnut halves

Preparation and cooking time: 20 minutes

1. In a small saucepan, combine honey and water. Stir over low heat until honey dissolves. Boil 2 minutes; add lemon juice, raisins and rum, if desired. Boil 5 minutes.
2. Place oranges in a medium bowl. Pour hot sauce over oranges. Let stand until cool. Cover and refrigerate.
3. Serve chilled. Decorate with walnuts. Makes 4 servings.

Clockwise from top left: Oranges in Raisin Syrup, Green Beans Greek-Style, Beef Paprika with Rice

Broccoli & Yogurt Salad

1-1/2 lb. broccoli, fresh or frozen
Salt
3/4 cup plain yogurt
2 teaspoons olive oil
1 teaspoon lemon juice
Freshly ground pepper
2 oz. mushrooms, thinly sliced
4 to 6 walnut halves

Preparation and cooking time: 25 minutes

1. Cut broccoli into 1-inch pieces. In a medium saucepan, cook broccoli in boiling, salted water until crisp-tender. Drain and cool.
2. To prepare dressing, in a small bowl, combine yogurt, olive oil, lemon juice, salt and pepper. If making ahead, refrigerate dressing and cooked broccoli in separate covered containers.
3. Place broccoli and mushrooms in a serving bowl. Add dressing. Toss lightly to combine; garnish with walnuts. Salad is best served cool but not cold. Makes 4 servings.

Stir-Fried Beef

1 lb. lean beef top-round steak
2 tablespoons soy sauce
4 teaspoons cornstarch
Salt
2 tablespoons vegetable oil
1 garlic clove, finely chopped
1 (1/2-inch) piece fresh gingerroot,
**   peeled, finely chopped**
1 cup chicken stock
2 tablespoons dry sherry
8 green onions, thinly sliced

Golden Rice:
1 cup uncooked long-grain white rice
1 teaspoon ground turmeric

To garnish:
2 green onions

Preparation and cooking time: 30 minutes, plus marinating

1. Trim excess fat from beef. Cut beef into thin slices; cut slices into 1/2-inch strips.
2. In a medium bowl, combine 1 tablespoon soy sauce, 1 teaspoon cornstarch and a pinch of salt. Add beef; toss to coat with marinade. Cover; let stand at room temperature 2 hours or refrigerate overnight. Drain beef, reserving marinade.
3. Heat oil in a large skillet or wok over medium-high heat. Add garlic and ginger; stir-fry 1 minute. Stir in marinated beef; stir-fry 2 minutes. Stir in stock, sherry and remaining soy sauce; bring to a boil. Reduce heat; simmer 10 minutes.
4. In a small bowl, combine remaining cornstarch and reserved marinade.
5. Stir cornstarch mixture and sliced green onions into beef mixture. Stir over low heat 1 to 2 minutes or until sauce thickens.
6. Prepare Golden Rice while beef is marinating. Cook rice and turmeric according to package directions. Spoon Golden Rice into a serving dish; spoon stir-fried beef mixture over rice. Garnish with green onions. Serve immediately. Makes 4 servings.

Strawberries in Butterscotch Sauce

1-1/2 lb. fresh or partially-thawed frozen strawberries
Sauce:
1 cup packed light-brown sugar
1 cup corn syrup
1/2 cup whipping cream
3 or 4 drops vanilla extract

Preparation and cooking time: 15 minutes

1. Place strawberries in individual serving dishes.
2. To prepare sauce, combine brown sugar and corn syrup in a medium saucepan. Stir over low heat until sugar dissolves. Cook 5 minutes.
3. Remove pan from heat; stir in cream and vanilla. Beat about 2 minutes or until sauce is smooth and glossy. Top strawberries with warm sauce. Or, make sauce ahead; refrigerate until served. Do not reheat; serve chilled. Makes 4 servings.

Clockwise from top left: Strawberries in Butterscotch Sauce, Broccoli & Yogurt Salad, Stir-Fried Beef with Golden Rice

Duck with Honey & Grape Sauce

4 duck quarters, weighing about 14 oz. each
Salt

Sauce:
1/4 cup honey
Grated peel and juice of 1/2 orange
8 oz. seedless grapes
1 tablespoon butter or margarine

To garnish:
Watercress sprigs

Preparation and cooking time: 1 hour 30 minutes

1. Preheat oven to 350F (175C). Prick duck pieces all over with a fork. Rub salt into skin. Place prepared duck, skin-side up, on a rack in a roasting pan.
2. Roast in preheated oven about 1-1/4 hours or until duck is tender and juices run clear when duck is pierced with a skewer.
3. While duck is roasting, in a small saucepan, combine honey, orange peel, orange juice, grapes and butter or margarine; bring to a boil.
4. Transfer duck to an ovenproof serving dish; pour sauce over duck; bake 5 minutes. Serve hot. Makes 4 servings.

Melon Balls in Ginger Sauce

1 medium cantaloupe or honeydew melon

Sauce:
8 oz. plain yogurt
4 teaspoons ginger syrup from preserved stem ginger
1 tablespoon finely chopped stem ginger
preserved in syrup
Pinch of grated nutmeg

To garnish:
4 orange slices

Preparation time: 20 minutes

1. Cut melon in half; scoop out and discard seeds. Using a melon baller or a small teaspoon, make melon balls. Place melon balls in a serving dish.
2. To prepare sauce, in a small bowl, combine yogurt, ginger syrup, stem ginger and nutmeg. Pour sauce over melon balls; stir to combine. Cover dish; refrigerate until served. Or, refrigerate melon balls and sauce separately. Place melon balls in individual serving dishes; top with sauce.
3. Garnish with orange slices. Makes 4 servings.

Nutty Cream Cones

1/4 cup butter or margarine, room temperature
1/4 cup sugar
1/3 cup all-purpose flour, sifted
1/8 teaspoon salt
1 egg, beaten

Cream Filling:
1/2 pint whipping cream (1 cup)
2 tablespoons powdered sugar
1/2 teaspoon vanilla extract
2 tablespoons toasted, chopped almonds
3 tablespoons toasted, sliced almonds

Preparation and cooking time: 50 minutes

1. Preheat oven to 400F (205C). Grease and flour 2 large baking sheets. Draw 8 (4-inch) circles on each sheet.
2. In a medium bowl, beat butter or margarine and sugar until light and fluffy. Fold in flour and salt. Stir in egg until thoroughly blended.
3. Drop 1-1/2 teaspoons batter into each circle on prepared baking sheets. Spread batter evenly with a small spatula to fill circles.
4. Bake in preheated oven, 1 baking sheet at a time, 4 minutes or until edges of cookies are golden.
5. Remove from oven; quickly shape each cookie around the handle of a wooden spoon to make a cone. Cool on spoon 1 minute. Remove from spoon; cool completely on a wire rack.
6. Repeat with remaining cookies. Cookies can be stored in airtight containers up to 2 days.
7. To make filling, in a medium bowl, whip cream until soft peaks form. Beat in powdered sugar and vanilla; beat until stiff peaks form. Fold in chopped almonds.
8. Spoon cream filling into rolled cookies; sprinkle with almonds. Makes 16 cones.

Top to bottom: Melon Balls in Ginger Sauce, Duck with Honey & Grape Sauce, Nutty Cream Cones

Curried Apple Soup
Whole-Wheat Spaghetti with Tuna Sauce
Green Salad
Blueberry Kissel

Whole-Wheat Spaghetti with Tuna Sauce

12 oz. whole-wheat spaghetti
1/4 cup butter or margarine
2 tablespoons olive oil
1 garlic clove, finely chopped
2/3 cup chicken stock
3 tablespoons dry sherry
1 (6-1/2-oz.) can tuna, drained, flaked
3 tablespoons chopped fresh parsley
Salt
Freshly ground pepper
2 tablespoons whipping cream

Preparation and cooking time: 30 minutes

1. Cook spaghetti according to package directions. Drain; return to pan. Stir in 1/2 of butter or margarine; keep warm.
2. Heat olive oil and remaining butter or margarine in a medium saucepan over medium heat. Add garlic; sauté 2 minutes. Stir in stock and sherry; boil 5 minutes to slightly reduce liquid. Stir in tuna and 2 tablespoons parsley. Season with salt and pepper; stir in cream.
3. Place spaghetti in a heated serving dish; add sauce. Toss to combine. Garnish with remaining parsley. Makes 4 servings.

Curried Apple Soup

3 tablespoons butter or margarine
1 lb. cooking apples, peeled, chopped
1 medium onion, sliced
2 celery stalks, thinly sliced
2 teaspoons curry powder
1 tablespoon chopped fresh mint
Juice of 1 lemon
2 cups chicken stock
2 tablespoons semolina
1-1/4 cups milk or plain yogurt
Salt
Freshly ground pepper

To garnish:
4 teaspoons shelled sunflower seeds
Chopped fresh parsley

Preparation and cooking time: 45 minutes

1. Melt butter or margarine in a large skillet over low heat. Add apples, onion and celery; cook 5 minutes, stirring occasionally. Increase heat to medium. Stir in curry powder; cook 3 minutes. Stir in mint, lemon juice and stock. Bring to a boil. Cover; simmer 20 minutes or until apples are tender.
2. In a blender or food processor fitted with a steel blade, process apple mixture until smooth. Place semolina in a medium saucepan; gradually stir in apple puree. Stir in milk or yogurt; bring slowly to a simmer. Do not boil. Season with salt and pepper.
3. Serve soup hot or refrigerate until chilled. Garnish with sunflower seeds and parsley. Makes 4 servings.

Clockwise from top left: Blueberry Kissel, Curried Apple Soup, Whole-Wheat Spaghetti with Tuna Sauce

Blueberry Kissel

1-1/2 lb. fresh or frozen blueberries
1/2 cup packed light-brown sugar
1/4 cup red wine
Juice and grated peel of 1/2 orange
1 tablespoon arrowroot or cornstarch
2 tablespoons granulated sugar

To serve:
1/4 cup toasted sliced almonds
Whipped cream
Cookies

Preparation and cooking time: 20 minutes

1. In a medium saucepan, combine blueberries, brown sugar, wine, orange juice and orange peel. Cook over low heat about 8 to 10 minutes or until blueberries are almost tender.
2. In a small bowl, stir a little juice from fruit into arrowroot or cornstarch to make a smooth paste. Stir into fruit; simmer about 2 minutes or until mixture thickens.
3. Pour blueberry mixture into a heatproof serving dish; sprinkle with granulated sugar to prevent a skin forming on top.
4. Arrange almonds decoratively over pudding. Serve warm or cold with whipped cream and cookies. Any leftover kissel makes a delicious sauce with ice cream. Makes 4 servings.

Fennel & Apple Salad
Chicken Breasts in Egg & Lemon Sauce
Long-Grain Brown Rice
Steamed Broccoli
Chocolate Pots with Cherry Brandy

Fennel & Apple Salad

2 medium fennel bulbs, trimmed, thinly sliced
2 Red Delicious apples, cored, thinly sliced
Dressing:
2/3 cup dairy sour cream
1 teaspoon cider vinegar
Grated peel of 1/2 orange
1 tablespoon orange juice
Pinch of sugar
Salt
Freshly ground pepper

To garnish:
2 tablespoons raisins

Preparation time: 15 minutes

1. Place fennel and apples in a serving bowl. Toss to combine.
2. To prepare dressing, in a small bowl, combine all ingredients. Spoon dressing over fennel and apples. Toss immediately to prevent browning of apples.
3. Garnish with raisins. Makes 4 servings.

Chicken Breasts in Egg & Lemon Sauce

4 chicken-breast halves, boneless
1 tablespoon vegetable oil
1/4 cup butter or margarine
4 oz. mushrooms, thinly sliced

Sauce:
2 tablespoons butter or margarine
2 tablespoons all-purpose flour
1 cup chicken stock
2 eggs
2 tablespoons lemon juice
1 tablespoon water
Salt
Freshly ground pepper

To garnish:
1 tablespoon chopped fresh parsley

Preparation and cooking time: 40 minutes

1. Remove skin from chicken; cut chicken on the diagonal into 3/4-inch slices. Heat oil and 1/4 cup butter or margarine in a large skillet over medium heat. Add chicken slices; sauté 4 minutes per side.
2. Add mushrooms; cook 4 minutes, turning chicken once. Remove chicken and mushrooms with a slotted spoon; keep warm.
3. To prepare sauce, melt 2 tablespoons butter or margarine in same skillet. Stir in flour; cook 1 minute. Gradually stir in stock; bring to a boil, stirring constantly. Reduce heat to low.
4. In a small bowl, beat eggs until frothy; beat in lemon juice and water.
5. Remove sauce from heat; add about 5 tablespoons hot sauce to beaten egg mixture. Stir mixture into sauce remaining in pan. Cook over low heat until sauce thickens; do not boil because sauce may curdle. Season with salt and pepper.
6. Add chicken and mushrooms to sauce; serve immediately. Garnish with parsley. Makes 4 servings.

Chocolate Pots with Cherry Brandy

1-1/2 cups half and half
4 oz. semisweet chocolate
4 egg yolks
1/4 cup sugar
1/8 teaspoon salt
2 tablespoons cherry-flavored brandy

To serve:
Cookies

Preparation and cooking time: 35 minutes, plus chilling

1. Heat half and half in a medium saucepan until tiny bubbles form around inside of saucepan. Do not boil.
2. Melt chocolate in top of a double boiler over simmering water. Remove from heat.
3. Add egg yolks to melted chocolate; beat until smooth. Stir in sugar and salt.
4. Gradually stir hot half and half into chocolate mixture. Return to heat; cook over simmering water about 15 minutes, stirring constantly. Stir in brandy.
5. Pour into 4 individual dessert dishes; set aside to cool. When cool, refrigerate several hours or until set.
6. Serve with cookies. Makes 4 servings.

Clockwise from left: Fennel & Apple Salad, Chocolate Pot with Cherry Brandy, Chicken Breasts in Egg & Lemon Sauce

Clockwise from left: Turkey Cutlets with Anchovies, Pear with Camembert Sauce, Pineapple Rings with Almond Meringue

---

Pears with Camembert Sauce
Turkey Cutlets with Anchovies
Broiled Tomatoes & Mushrooms
Pineapple Rings with Almond Meringue

Pears with Camembert Sauce

4 ripe dessert pears, peeled, halved, cored
1 tablespoon lemon juice
1/2 cup dairy sour cream
2 tablespoons whipping cream
2 oz. Camembert cheese, room temperature
Pinch of red (cayenne) pepper

To garnish:
Mint sprigs

Preparation time: 15 minutes

1. Brush pear with lemon juice to prevent browning; arrange pears, cut-side up, in a shallow serving dish.
2. In a blender or food processor fitted with a steel blade, process sour cream, whipping cream, cheese and red pepper until smooth.
3. Top each pear with sauce; garnish with mint. Makes 4 servings.

Turkey Cutlets with Anchovies

Juice of 1 lemon
2 tablespoons vegetable oil
1 teaspoon dried leaf oregano
Salt
Freshly ground pepper
4 turkey-breast cutlets, about 4 oz. each
2 tablespoons all-purpose flour
1-1/2 cups fresh bread crumbs
Grated peel of 1 lemon
2 tablespoons chopped fresh mint or parsley
1 egg
1 tablespoon milk
1/4 cup vegetable oil for sautéing

To garnish:
8 anchovy fillets
8 pimento-stuffed green olives
2 hard-cooked eggs, sliced

Preparation and cooking time: 30 minutes, plus marinating

1. In a shallow dish, combine lemon juice, 2 tablespoons oil, oregano, salt and pepper. Add turkey cutlets; turn to coat. Cover; marinate 1 hour at room temperature or overnight in refrigerator, turning once.
2. Drain marinated turkey; pat dry with paper towels. In a shallow dish, combine flour, salt and pepper. Dip turkey into seasoned flour to coat.
3. In another shallow dish, combine bread crumbs, lemon peel and mint or parsley. In another shallow dish, beat egg and milk until combined.
4. Dip floured turkey slices into egg mixture, then into bread-crumb mixture.
5. Heat 1/4 cup oil in a large skillet over medium heat. Add coated turkey cutlets; sauté 3 to 4 minutes per side or until golden brown.
6. Arrange cooked cutlets on a heated serving dish. Roll anchovies around olives. Garnish cutlets with olives and hard-cooked-egg slices. Serve hot. Makes 4 servings.

Pineapple Rings with Almond Meringue

8 (1/2-inch-thick) fresh or canned pineapple slices
3 tablespoons butter or margarine, melted
2 tablespoons dark rum

Meringue:
2 egg whites
1/2 cup packed light-brown sugar
1/2 cup ground almonds

Preparation and cooking time: 30 minutes

1. Preheat broiler. Drain canned pineapple, if using; pat dry with paper towels. Place on a broiler-pan rack. Brush pineapple slices on 1 side with 1/2 of butter or margarine.
2. Broil under preheated broiler 4 minutes. Turn pineapple; brush with remaining butter or margarine. Broil 3 to 4 minutes or until pineapple is lightly browned and bubbling. Brush with rum.
3. In a medium bowl, beat egg whites until soft peaks form. Gradually beat in sugar until stiff and glossy. Fold in ground almonds.
4. Spoon meringue mixture over rings; with back of a spoon, make peaks in meringue. Broil 2 minutes or until lightly browned. Serve immediately. Makes 4 servings.

Variation
Substitute 2/3 cup shredded coconut for ground almonds. Sprinkle extra coconut over meringue before broiling. The coconut forms a crisp, toasted crust that contrasts perfectly with the soft, chewy meringue.

> *Potato & Sausage Salad*
> *Leek & Cheese Flan*
> *Tomatoes*
> *Hot French Bread*
> *Baked Apples with Apricot*

Potato & Sausage Salad

1 lb. new potatoes
Salt
6 to 8 green onions, thinly sliced
2 tablespoons chopped chives
1 tablespoon chopped chervil or fresh parsley
1/2 cup dairy sour cream
1 tablespoon white-wine vinegar
Freshly ground pepper
6 oz. summer sausage, in 1 piece

Preparation and cooking time: 40 minutes

1. In a large saucepan, cook potatoes in boiling, salted water until tender. Drain; let stand until cool enough to handle. Peel; cut into thick slices or quarter.
2. In a medium bowl, combine onions, herbs and sour cream; stir in vinegar and pepper. Stir in potatoes until coated.
3. Remove and discard skin from sausage; cut in 1/2-inch cubes. If making ahead, refrigerate potato salad and sausage cubes in separate covered containers.
4. Immediately before serving, stir sausage cubes into potato salad. Makes 4 servings.

Leek & Cheese Flan

1-1/4 cups all-purpose flour
1/2 teaspoon salt
6 tablespoons chilled shortening
3 to 4 tablespoons iced water

Filling:
2 tablespoons butter or margarine
4 medium leeks, thinly sliced
1 tablespoon snipped chives
1 cup shredded Swiss, Gruyère or Cheddar cheese (4 oz.)
3 eggs
1-1/2 cups half and half
Salt
Freshly ground pepper

To serve:
Tomato halves

Preparation and cooking time: 1 hour

1. Combine flour and salt in a medium bowl. With a pastry blender or 2 knives, cut in shortening until mixture resembles coarse crumbs.
2. Sprinkle with 3 tablespoons water; toss with a fork until mixture begins to hold together. Add remaining water, if necessary. Gather dough into a ball; shape into a flattened round. Wrap in plastic wrap; refrigerate 30 minutes.
3. Preheat oven to 400F (205C).
4. On a lightly floured surface, roll out dough to a 12-inch circle. Use pastry to line a 9-inch quiche or flan pan with a removable bottom. Trim pastry edge. Prick bottom and side of pastry with a fork. Line with foil; fill foil with pie weights or dried beans.
5. Bake 10 minutes. Remove foil and pie weights; bake 5 minutes. Reduce oven temperature to 375F (190C).
6. To prepare filling, melt butter or margarine in a medium skillet. Add leeks; sauté 4 minutes. With a slotted spoon, transfer cooked leeks to baked pie crust. Sprinkle with chives and 1/2 of cheese.
7. In a medium bowl, beat eggs, half and half, salt and pepper until blended. Pour over leeks and cheese. Sprinkle with remaining cheese.
8. Bake 30 to 35 minutes or until center is set. Serve warm. For a special touch, cut tomato halves with a zigzag cutter. Makes 6 servings.